AA

Explore Britain's

NATIONAL PARKS

D1318450

The Automobile Association
Fanum House, Basingstoke, Hampshire RG21 2EA

AA

Explore Britain's
NATIONAL
PARKS

by Roland Smith

Foreword by Chris Bonington CBE

Copy Editor: Rebecca Snelling

Published by The Automobile Association, Fanum House, Basingstoke, Hampshire RG21 2EA

Published in the US by Hunter Publishing, Inc., 300 Raritan Center Parkway, Edison, NJ 08818.
ISBN 1-55650-594-9

A catalogue record for this book is available from the British Library.

ISBN h/b 0 7495 0683 0
      s/b 0 7495 0773 X

This book was produced using QuarkXPress™, Aldus Freehand™ and MicrosoftWord™ on Apple Macintosh™ computers.

Colour origination by L.C. Repro and Sons Ltd, Aldermaston.
Printed and bound by Butler and Tanner Ltd, Frome and London.

The contents of this book are believed correct at the time of printing. Nevertheless, the Publishers cannot accept responsibility for errors or omissions, or for changes in details given.

Acknowledgements: The Automobile Association wishes to thank the following photographers and libraries for their assistance in the preparation of this book:

AA PHOTO LIBRARY with contributions from F/Cover & Spine A.Lawson, B/Cover J.Morrison, B/Cover P.Baker, 6/7 E.Roberts, 8a R.Newton, 8b A.Lawson, 8c H.Williams, 8d S&O Matthews, 10 E.Bowness, 12, 13 H.Williams, 14 S.Gregory, 15 A.Baker, 16 J.Beazley, 17 P.Baker, 18/9 J.Wyand, 20, 21 J.Wyand, 22 A.Lawson, 23, 24, 25, 26 A.Lawson, 27 J.Wyand, 28, 29 A.Lawson, 30/1 T.Teegan, 32 A.Lawson, 33 H.Williams, 35 A.Lawson, 37 S&O Matthews, 38 T.Teegan, 39, 40 H.Williams, 41 A.Lawson, 42/3, 44 C&A Molyneux, 45 H.Williams, 46, 47 C&A.Molyneux, 48/9 I.Burgum, 50, 51, 52, C&A Molyneux, 53 H.Williams, 54/5 M.Allwood-Coppin, 56 J.Gravell, 57, 58 C&A Molyneux, 59 H.Williams, 62 C.Molyneux, 63 J.Gravell, 64 M.Adelman, 65 J.Gravell, 66/7 D.Croucher, 68 E.Roberts, 69 D.Croucher, 70 R.Newton, 71 A.Hopkins, 72 D.Croucher, 73 T.Timms, 74 R.Newton, 75, 76 M.Allwood-Coppin, 77 R.Newton, 78/9 A.Tryner, 80, 81 M.Birkitt, 83, 84, 85 P.Baker, 86 A.Tryner, 87 P.Baker, 88 A.Tryner, 89, 90 P.Baker, 91 A.Tryner, 92/3 H.Williams, 94 A.Hopkins, 95 A.Baker, 96, 97, 98, 99 J.Morrison, 100 A.Hopkins, 101, 102 A.Baker, 104/5, 106, 107, 108, 109, 112, 113, 114, 115, 116, 117, 118/9, P.Sharp, 120 S.Gregory, 121 H.Williams, 122, 123, 124/5 P.Baker, 124 G.Rowatt, 126, 127, 128, 129, S.Gregory, 130/1 S&O Matthews, 132, 133 D.Forss, 134, 135, 136, 138, 139, 140, 141 J.Beazley, 143 A.Perkins, 144 A.Souter, 145, 146 A.Perkins, 147 S&O Matthews, 148, 149, 150 A.Perkins, 151 S&O Matthews, 152, 153 P.Baker, 154 H.Williams, 155 S&O Matthews, 156 J.Carnie, 157 J.Beazley, 158 J.Carnie, 159 K.Paterson
THE MANSELL COLLECTION 110a S.T Coleridge, 110b William Wordsworth, 111a John Ruskin
MARY EVANS PICTURE LIBRARY 111b Beatrix Potter

CONTENTS

FOREWORD

The snow-clad peaks, about 10 miles distant, had the majesty of Everest and to a 17-year-old who had never before ventured into mountainous country, they were as challenging. This was my first view of Snowdon, 42 years ago, after hitch-hiking up the A5 from London to Capel Curig in North Wales and coming round the corner of what was then the Royal Hotel. I find that view as beautiful and inspiring today as I did all those years ago. In that period I have visited and climbed in most of Britain's National Parks, h**ave** lived in the Lake District for 25 years, and have come to cherish and understand the significance of the Parks, both as a visitor and a resident.

Our National Parks are very different from those of America for they are not wilderness areas. People have lived in the British parks since earliest times. Even the remotest hill country has been affected by man, the grass cropped short by grazing sheep, dry stone walls snake across the fells and barns or houses nestle in the valleys. It doesn't matter where you travel, to the great peaks of the Himalaya, the ice-filled fjords of Eastern

Snow-capped peaks rise over Nant
Gwynedd, Snowdonia

Greenland or the empty fastness of Antarctica, there is nowhere more beautiful or varied than the British countryside. It is the tonal and textural variety of colouring of the foliage and rock, the quality of the light and the variety of the forms that make it so special. On a stormy winter's day, when the mountains are blanketed in snow and wreathed in cloud, it can seem like the wildest place on earth. Yet on a clear, balmy summer's evening, with the hills lit by the warm glow of the setting sun and cottages gleaming white in the valley below, the very same place takes on a soft, gentle beauty. The hand of man has, in the main, been harmonious but the pressures imposed by an ever-increasing number of visitors and modern development has undoubtedly threatened some of our most outstanding unspoilt scenery.

Effective long term planning was becoming increasingly important. The introduction of National Parks in the early 1950s was an essential step in giving protection to some of the most beautiful country in Britain and the means for local communities to develop and prosper in a way that is sympathetic with the natural environment.

The pressure today is greater than it has ever been. You can see it in the car-choked roads and in the broad, eroded swathes across hillsides caused by thousands of feet. Yet free access to our countryside is vitally important to people living in an increasingly pressured and complex society. It is only by careful, sensitive, yet firm planning that the many demands on this fragile environment can be balanced out, not just for us today but for future generations as well.

CHRIS BONINGTON
President, Council for National Parks

USEFUL INFORMATION

All of the National Parks run information centres, from which you can
obtain books and leaflets. Some of
the centres are open only during the
summer months. For further details
and for other information contact the
addresses below.

Brecon Beacons National Park
7 Glamorgan Street
Brecon
Powys LD3 7DP
Tel (0874) 624437

The Broads
Broads Authority
Thomas Harvey House
18 Colegate
Norwich
Norfolk NR3 1BQ
Tel (0603) 610734

Dartmoor National Park
Parke
Haytor Road
Bovey Tracey
Devon TQ13 9JQ
Tel (0626) 832093

Exmoor National Park
Exmoor House
Dulverton
Somerset TA22 9HL
Tel (0398) 23665

Lake District National Park
Brockhole
Windermere
Cumbria LA23 1LJ
Tel (05394) 46601

The New Forest
New Forest Committee
Queen's House
Lyndhurst
Hampshire SO43 7NH
Tel (0703) 284144

North York Moors National Park
The Old Vicarage
Bondgate
Helmsley
York YO6 5BP
Tel (0439) 70657

Northumberland National Park
Eastburn
South Park
Hexham
Northumberland NE36 1BS
Tel (0434) 605555

Peak National Park
Aldern House
Baslow Road
Bakewell
Derbyshire DE45 1AE
Tel (0629) 814321

Pembrokeshire Coast National Park
County Offices
Haverfordwest
Dyfed SA61 1QZ
Tel (0437) 764591

Snowdonia National Park
Penrhyndeudraeth
Gwynedd LL48 6LS
Tel (0766) 770274

Yorkshire Dales National Park
Colvend
Hebden Road
Grassington
Skipton
North Yorkshire BD23 5LB
Tel (0756) 752748

All the National Parks have their own decorative signs

SCOTLAND

Northumberland

NEWCASTLE

Lake
District

North
York Moors

Yorkshire
Dales

YORK

LEEDS

MANCHESTER

SHEFFIELD

Snowdonia

Peak
District

NORWICH

Norfolk
Broads

BIRMINGHAM

ENGLAND

WALES

Brecon
Beacons

Pembrokeshire
Coast

CARDIFF

BRISTOL

LONDON

Exmoor

SOUTHAMPTON

New
Forest

Dartmoor

PLYMOUTH

0	20	40	60	80	100 miles
0	40	80	120	160 km.

Snow-capped Skiddaw from Ashness Bridge, in the Lake District

INTRODUCTION

The Great Outdoors

According to the latest official surveys, a day out in the country – with perhaps a walk of 2 miles (3.2km) or more – is Britain's number one outdoor attraction – more popular even than going to a football match, angling or golf.

This huge boom in the popularity of walking in the country has meant that more and more people are donning their boots and heading for the great outdoors, and where better to do that than in the National Parks? These officially designated jewels in our countryside crown received over 100 million day visits in 1991, and, with the increased leisure-time people find they have for various reasons, there can be no doubt that these figures are bound to rise even higher as we approach the turn of the century.

Britain's 11 National Parks cover ten per cent of the land surface of England and Wales – there are none in Scotland – but, astonishingly, 40 years after their inception and despite being among the nation's best-loved landscapes, our National Parks still suffer from an acute identity problem.

Despite the name, they are neither 'national' in the sense of being owned by the nation, nor 'parks' in the normally accepted, urban 'keep-off-the-grass' sense. Often confused with the National Trust (the registered charity which has similar aims and which owns large parts of several of the Parks), the National Parks have still not established themselves as part of the nation's culture as they have, say, in the USA. Admittedly, they have been established in the States for over a century, as opposed to 40-odd years in Britain.

So what is a National Park? Put simply, it is a substantial area of outstanding countryside which has been set aside by Parliament for special protection because of its scenic beauty. National Park designation does not change any land ownership rights, nor does it normally allow any special rights of access to the public. The same laws of the land apply to National Parks just as they do anywhere else in the country, so the visitor enjoys no special privileges while in the Parks and should therefore respect the property and rights of local people just as he would anywhere else.

Despite the definition of a National Park, visitors can be confused by the title, and National Park authorities constantly receive queries such as: 'When does the Park close?' and 'Where are the wild animals?'.

A National Park authority's main task is to act as the local planning committee, controlling development in the Park and trying to ensure that harmful change does not take place, so that future generations can enjoy the landscape as much as we do today. There is, however, much more to their remit than that. The authorities are also charged with providing suitable open-air recreational opportunities for their visitors, and with protecting the wildlife and historic heritage of the Parks while paying due regard to the interests of the 250,000 people who live and work in the National Parks. This is an incredibly difficult balancing act, a constant see-saw of conflicting claims and counter-claims which means the National Park authorities often just cannot win. That unsightly limestone quarry eating into the hillside may be an intolerable blot on the landscape to the conservationist, but to the local family whose breadwinner is employed there, or to the village store which provides for those who work there it is an absolutely vital element of the local economy. That new road which is urgently needed to relieve congestion or to transport goods more quickly and easily between cities is a 'must' for the road haulage lobby, but does it have to slice through a wild and beautiful area which has been set aside as a National Park, bringing with it the unwelcome sights, sounds and smells of a snarling urban motorway?

Also, despite the 'peace dividend', we know that the military must have somewhere to train and that pilots must have somewhere to practise their low-level flying skills and that the best place to do it is in the hills, where the population is sparse. However, it still comes as something of a shock to read a notice in a National Park which says: 'Do Not Touch Anything. It May Explode And Kill You', or to be awakened from your reverie as you triumphantly crest the top of a heather-clad hill by the thunderous, ear-shattering sound of a contour-hugging supersonic jet fighter. The Parks are, after all, areas which Parliament has officially designated as places for 'quiet, open-air enjoyment' for the people.

One insuperable problem is that the Parks' twin aims of conservation and recreation – two equally laudable objectives – often conflict with one another. Allowing free access to open moorland, for example, may be the Holy Grail for ramblers, some of whom in the past have even gone to prison to exercise that cherished 'right to roam', but to the ecologist that same stretch of open moorland is the breeding ground for rare birds of prey, such as the merlin and the hen harrier, and allowing free access to walkers could cause serious disturbance to this wildlife.

The National Park authorities are constantly called upon to make these

Malmsmead, in the heart of Exmoor's Lorna Doone Country

kinds of difficult decisions, but when it comes to the crunch Parliament has decreed that the conservation of these beautiful and precious, yet fragile, landscapes must always come first – although Governments of all political persuasions sometimes still inexcusably forget the fact.

About 75 per cent of the expenditure of the National Park authorities comes directly from the Government by means of a special grant, which in 1990/91 totalled roughly £18.75 million for all 11 Parks – less than the annual grant given to the Royal Opera House, Convent Garden. It is also much less than the cost of one of those low-flying jet fighters which so regularly shatter the peace of the Parks. Despite the long-term importance of their work, and the pleasure they give to millions, most National Parks survive on much the same kind of budget as a medium-sized comprehensive school.

The other 25 per cent of National Parks' expenditure comes from a precept on the local authority within which the National Park falls. In return for this the Park authority carries out the local planning function of those authorities. Increasingly, National Park authorities are generating their own income by other means such as sales from visitor centres, other commercial activities, and charges for specialist services.

National Park authorities are often accused by their critics of being undemocratic and of being controlled by unelected outsiders. The truth is that the constitution of National Park authorities is laid down by law, which states that two-thirds of the decision-making executive membership must be drawn from local county and district councils, and the remaining one-third are to be directly appointed by the Government. The latter are nominally appointed to look after the national interest, but in fact are increasingly chosen from among the local population.

Breakers crash against the rocks of Mill Bay, on the Pembrokeshire coast

Gormire Lake and the Plain of York from Sutton Bank, North York Moors

The story of British National Parks, and of the international National Parks movement, began in perhaps the best-known Park – the Lake District. In his *Guide Through the District of the Lakes in the North of England*, one of the first tourist guides to the area, published in 1810, William Wordsworth first suggested that 'persons of pure taste' should join him in deeming that the district should be 'a sort of national property, in which every man has a right and interest who has an eye to perceive and a heart to enjoy'.

Sixty-two years later, in 1872, the first National Park in the world was set up by far-sighted, gun-toting pioneers at Yellowstone on the borders of Montana and Wyoming, in the United States. However, the uninhabited, State-owned wildernesses that more extensive countries such as America can afford to set aside as National Parks bear little resemblance to the privately-owned, lived-in areas of countryside of Britain, where every square mile of land normally has several different uses and claims upon it, all of particular importance to one group or another.

It was to take another lifetime of campaigning and two world wars before the blueprint for Britain's system of National Parks was finally laid down. In between there were several disappointments, a catalogue of broken promises and a number of often bitter confrontations. William Wordsworth was the first of the upper middle-class, somewhat elitist preservationists, whose greatest dread was that their beloved Lakes would be destroyed if 'artisans, labourers and the humbler class of shopkeepers' were allowed to come and enjoy it. Yet it was from this privileged class that the impetus came for National Park legislation, first from James (later Lord) Bryce's Access to Mountains Bill of 1884, and then Charles (later Lord) Trevelyan's similarly titled bill of 1908, which he followed with three more attempts, all of which were ultimately withdrawn. Later the Addison Committee of 1931 reported on the desirability of setting aside National Parks in Britain, but the next important catalyst for the National Park movement came from an entirely different source. The 1930s were a time of deep depression and widespread unemployment, and for the people living in the large industrial cities of the north of England weekend rambles on the moors became a vital means of relaxation. But many of the highest, wildest and most attractive moors were forbidden to the public at this time because they were the exclusive domain of their grouse-shooting owners, and strictly policed by burly gamekeepers. The whole situation came to a head in the Peak District in April 1932 when the celebrated Mass Trespass on Kinder Scout took place.

Five 'ramblers from Manchester way'(as they were described) were sent to prison for their part in this event, which has now entered rambling folklore, but they lit a torch for National Parks and access to the countryside which was to burn ever more fiercely throughout the long years of World War II.

The post-war Labour Government was committed to the outdoor cause in a way that no other Government has been before or since. Members of the Cabinet regularly went for walks along the proposed line of the Pennine Way with Tom Stephenson, a campaigning journalist who had joined the Ministry of Town and Country Planning as Press Officer in 1943. He later recalled that the only kindred spirit among the civil servants there was John Dower, a consumptive young architect and town planner who, in 1945, was given the task of writing the report which was to create the blueprint for the British National Parks system. The Dower Report, as it is known, remains one of the most visionary documents ever to appear in the forbidding covers of a Government command paper, and in it Dower outlined the generally accepted definition of a British-style National Park. It was, he wrote:

Limestone crags and scree in Lathkill Dale, in White Peak country

...an extensive area of beautiful and relatively wild country in which, for the national benefit and by appropriate national decision and action, (a) the characteristic landscape beauty is strictly preserved, (b) access and facilities for public open-air enjoyment are amply provided, (c) wildlife and buildings and places of architectural and historic interest are suitably protected, while (d) established farming use is effectively maintained.

Dower proposed that ten National Parks should be set up within five years and when Sir Arthur Hobhouse, Chairman of the National Parks Committee, reported two years later, Dower's definition was ratified and 12 Parks (including the Broads and the South Downs) were proposed along with an administration system which was incorporated in the long-awaited National Parks and Access to the Countryside Act of 1949. Although the legislation fell far short of the hopes of some of the pioneers, at least it was on the statute book.

During the next six years ten National Parks were designated, although only the first two, the Peak and the Lakes, were administered by the independent planning boards proposed by Dower and Hobhouse. The others – Snowdonia, Dartmoor, Pembrokeshire Coast, North York Moors, Yorkshire Dales, Exmoor, Northumberland and the Brecon Beacons – were all run by special committees of the county councils within whose jurisdiction they fell. The Norfolk and Suffolk Broads eventually joined the family as a National Park in all but name, after a gap of 32 years, in 1989, and the Government has recently announced that the New Forest will soon be similarly designated as an independent authority. However, the Government has so far resisted grasping the nettle with regard to designating National Parks in Scotland, as Dower had hoped they might, preferring voluntary conservation agreements instead.

In 1984, the Countryside Commission, which succeeded the National Parks Commission as the Government body responsible for National Parks in 1968, initiated a two-year National Parks Awareness

Hadrian's Wall marches across Housesteads Crag, Northumberland

Campaign in partnership with the Park authorities. The idea was to make the British public more aware of their heritage of National Parks, and the politicians more supportive of them. The campaign culminated in 1987 with a National Parks Festival at Chatsworth in the Peak District which was attended by the Princess of Wales, Ministers and 15,000 people.

Over the past 40 years, despite being starved of resources and falling victim to inconsistent Governmental decisions, the National Parks have generally managed to hold that thin green line successfully. But what does the future hold for them? Supporters were heartened by the Government's general acceptance of the Edwards Report of 1991, which was the first major review of the working of the National Parks for 15 years. Entitled *Fit for the Future*, the report proposed that all Parks should revert to being administered by independent boards, and that the purposes of the Parks should be redefined to refer expressly to 'quiet enjoyment and under-standing, and to the conservation of the wildlife and cultural heritage'.

There can be no doubt that many of the existing Parks are in grave danger of being too popular for their own good as more and more people seek out their beauty and solitude in this increasingly overcrowded and pressurised island of ours. However, we can be certain that, even if they are not always easily accessible, the National Parks will remain as precious pockets of unspoilt land with a safe future, although it remains to be seen whether the idealistic and egalitarian dreams of early National Park pioneers like Trevelyan, Dower, Hobhouse and Stephenson will ever be fulfilled.

One thing is certain – the snobbish elitism favoured by Wordsworth has not survived. As the architect of the National Parks, John Dower, wrote nearly half a century ago:

National Parks are not for any privileged or otherwise restricted section of the population, but for all who care to refresh their minds and spirits and to exercise their bodies in a peaceful setting of natural beauty.

Part of the next National Park – the Beaulieu River on the eastern edge of the New Forest

DARTMOOR

Dartmoor is often dubbed the last wilderness of southern Britain, but wilderness is a relative term and although the 368 square mile (953 sq km) National Park appears at first sight to consist of an open, bleak, moorland core crossed by few roads, everywhere you look reveals evidence of human presence. Nowhere in north-western Europe has a greater density of prehistoric remains, and nowhere in Britain can you feel the same brooding sense of a past extending over 5,000 years.

*Previous pages, the granite
bastions of Houndtor,
Dartmoor National Park*

*Bronze Age Dartmoor – the
remains of a hut circle at
Grimspound*

Now I am no horseman, so I approached the pony-trekking trip across the heart of Dartmoor with some trepidation. But I needn't have worried. Our mounts were almost boringly docile, and seemed to know every hoofprint of the way between Manaton, on the eastern side of the moor, and our lunch stop at the Warren House Inn, where the roaring open fire in the bar is said to have been kept burning for a hundred years - a testimony to the bleakness of its situation.

We began our excursion by climbing up from the conifer belts of Natsworthy, following the ridge above the East Webburn River between Hameldown Tor and Hookney Tor. The haul had been long and slow, but as we breasted the col between the tors, and the Challacombe valley was revealed below, we looked down on a landscape which was the epitome of Dartmoor. In the foreground, encircled by a heather-covered bank, was Grimspound, perhaps the most complete Bronze Age village site in England. The circular hut sites lined with granite moorstone stood out clearly in the dark, chocolate-brown heather, while on the rugged tors above, cairns and tumuli – marked by Gothic lettering on the map – showed where the chieftains of this long-deserted village were buried perhaps

4,000 years ago. In front of us, on the moorland slopes above the enclosures of the 18th-century Headland Warren Farm, the extensive remains of the East Birch Tor Tin Mine indicated where the miners of the 16th century and earlier had dug for the ore, cutting deep, ravine-like gullies into the moor. Below us, in the valley of the West Webburn, the many parallel ridges showed where the miners had streamed for alluvial tin, in much the same way as gold prospectors panned for gold. A straighter, sharp-sided and more continuous gully running the length of the valley marked the course of a leat, or artificial water channel, which had fed a large waterwheel whose pit was still visible in the valley bottom. This wheel powered the pumping rods which drained the East Birch Tor Tin Mine back in the mid-19th century.

The name Headland Warren is a clue to another medieval occupation on Dartmoor. From those times until as late as the mid-20th century rabbits were bred in artificial warrens for their meat, and Headland Warren was one of the biggest. In other places strange cigar-shaped mounds, easily confused with Bronze Age barrows and known to the archaeologist as pillow mounds, show where artificial burrows were made to encourage the rabbits to breed. Further down the valley, on the slopes of Challacombe Down, the distinct lines of parallel terraces could be made out running north–south across the hillside. These were the remains of medieval strip lynchets, created by the build-up of oxen-ploughed soil against the boundaries of the ancient fields which contoured across the hillside. Narrower corrugations within some of them

A farmstead nestles in the lee of the moor, deep in the heart of Dartmoor

*The reconstructed clapper
bridge at Postbridge*

marked the ridge-and-furrow of further medieval cultivations. With more hut circles further down the West Webburn valley and on Challacombe Down, and the remains of a prehistoric stone row marching up its northern flank through the open-cast tin workings, the view was a perfect example of what is known as the Dartmoor palimpsest – layer upon layer of human artefacts fossilised in the modern landscape.

You can expect to see many, if not all, of these features during the course of a typical afternoon's walk on Dartmoor, the prehistoric metropolis of our National Parks, and to find the reason for the amazingly complete preservation of the historic features we must look at Dartmoor's geology.

Dartmoor is the last knuckle in a Cyclopean underground granite fist which extends across the West Country from Land's End through Bodmin Moor. About 280 million years ago molten granite forced its way up through the younger, sedimentary rocks above and cooled slowly to form the rough, grey granite we see in the

tors and boulder-strewn valley slopes today. Most of the prehistoric monuments, from the stone circles to the stone rows and territorial boundaries known as reaves which run ruler-straight for mile after mile across the moor, were built of this enduring stone. Perhaps the most impressive natural landforms on the sweeping, sepia-brown moor where the ever-changing shafts of light constantly open up new vistas are those weird, roughly-weathered tors. The name comes from the Old English *torr*, meaning a high rock, and Dartmoor's tors are probably more famous than their millstone grit counterparts in the Pennines. Perhaps the best-known are the massive Hay Tor, looking like the wrinkled back of a sitting elephant on the eastern side of the moor above Bovey Tracey, and nearby Hound Tor, a wild collection of rocks with the well-preserved remains of a medieval village nestling among the bracken and boulder clitter at its foot. One of the strangest tors is the 20ft (6m) high natural rock sculpture of Bowerman's Nose, on Hayne Down

above Manaton. Some people have whimsically likened this artificial-looking pile of granite building blocks to the cartoon character Andy Capp, while others have sensed a much more primitive, primeval presence.

On the opposite side of the great plateau of the moor, Great Mis Tor, Yes Tor and the 100ft (30m) high, lichen-encrusted pile of Vixen Tor look down on the birthplace of the River Tavy. All the tors are different and highly individual, yet all were formed in the same way. After years of discussion about their origin, most experts now seem to agree that they are the result of high bosses of granite being exposed to the weathering agents of ice, frost, wind and rain for centuries. Eventually the joints were prised open, leaving the upstanding masses of rock we see today.

Combstone Tor, typical of Dartmoor's granite outcrops

Dartmoor obviously takes its name from the fact that it is the birthplace of the great River Dart, and the West and East Dart merge at Dartmeet to flow south then east through the pleasant abbey town of Buckfastleigh, eventually entering the English Channel at the port of Dartmouth. The only Dartmoor rivers to head north to the Bristol Channel are the West and East Okements, which meet at Okehampton on the northern edge of the moor. The natural vegetation cover of the moor after the Ice Age and until man began to clear it in Neolithic times was forest. This has been proved by analysis of the large areas of peat covering the highest points of the moor, where the pollen remains of oak, birch, elm and hazel are common. The only places where the visitor can still experience that primeval wildwood are in precious, protected remnants such as Wistman's Wood, on the slopes of the West Dart near Two Bridges, or Black Tor Beare in the West Okement valley above the Meldon Reservoir.

These are among my favourite places on Dartmoor, where the most

The West Dart River, one of the major rivers in this area, near Hexworthy

fantastically stunted and gnarled pendunculate oaks grow straight from the chaotic boulder clitter. Trees and rocks are festooned with dripping grey-green lichens and ferns, creating an enchanted, fairy-tale landscape. They always remind me of an Arthur Rackham illustration, and if you are there on a misty, autumnal day you wouldn't be the least surprised to see one of Dartmoor's fabled pixies popping up from behind the nearest boulder to pass the time of day.

The wildlife of Dartmoor is strictly limited to those species which can adapt to the harsh and often wet conditions of the moor. With an annual rainfall averaging over 60in (152.5cm), and a high risk of snowfall in the winter because of its 2000ft (610m) altitude, Dartmoor is not always the most hospitable of habitats. One magical feature of Dartmoor, caused by its cold, wet winter climate, is the rare ammil, when every leaf, twig and rock is sheathed in a thin layer of ice. If the wind gets up, you may be treated to the ethereal sound of a thousand icy cymbals gently clashing together.

Most famous of Dartmoor's animals is, of course, the wild-maned Dartmoor pony, chosen as the symbol of the National Park authority. Dartmoor ponies are well-known to picnickers for their roadside scavenging, but the Park authority warns against feeding these semi-wild animals. First mentioned in the will of the Saxon Bishop Aelfwold of Crediton, they are thought to have descended from stock released on the

Enchanted Wistman's Wood, near Two Bridges, a remnant of Dartmoor's wildwood

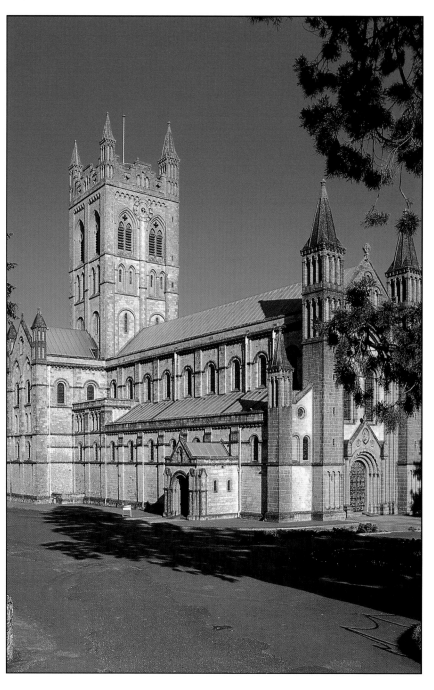

Buckfast Abbey, rebuilt by Benedictine monks and completed in 1937

moor during the Dark Ages. The best time to see them is during the annual autumnal gatherings, or drifts, when they are rounded up and branded.

The mewing cry of the buzzard or the harsh bark of the raven are often the only signs of birdlife on moorland rambles, while the birdlife in the well-wooded valleys, or coombes, which surround the moor is much richer. Here you can expect to see in summer such species as pied flycatcher, wood warbler and redstart, and from the animal world, the occasional roe deer, badger, fox, and even, if you are extremely lucky, an otter. Some of these wild, woodland animals were undoubtedly among the prey of the first hunter-gatherers who moved in from the coast and first started the clearance of the forested moor. We have already seen how, in prehistoric times, the moor was much more heavily populated than it is today. At least 5,000 hut circles, mainly dating from the Bronze Age, have so far been indentified on the moor, and more evidence of a large and settled resident population is found each year.

A deterioration in the climate from 1000 to 500BC saw the gradual depopulation of the high moor, and the only surviving evidence from the Dark Ages seems to be a ring of Iron

Age hillforts encircling the western approaches of the moor. The settlement pattern which now exists on Dartmoor largely stems from the Saxon and medieval periods when the mineral wealth of the moor, and in particular the discovery of tin ore, or cassiterite, caused another period of intense human activity. Almost everywhere you look on the moor there are the remains of this industrial boom, from the streamworks mentioned previously to the isolated tinners' huts at the heart of the moor.

The tin workers were governed by the so-called Stannary Court, which administered a harsh justice on wrong-doers.The stannary towns, where the ore was assayed, bought and sold, included Ashburton and Chagford within the Park. Lydford was the administrative centre, where the laws were enforced and the luckier offenders finished up in the stern, square-walled Lydford Castle after the application of so-called 'Lydford Law'. Dreaded by generations of Dartmoor people, it is recalled in the doggerel verse:

'First hang and draw
Then hear the cause, is Lydford Law.'

The wealth won from tin, and later copper, silver, lead, and most recently the enormous china clay quarries at Lee Moor at the south-western corner of the Park, brought prosperity to the

A Dartmoor pony grazes peacefully on the open moor above Tavistock

moor dwellers. This is reflected in the fine granite-towered churches at places like Widecombe-in-the-Moor, Lydford and Moretonhampstead, and the lovely old traditional Dartmoor longhouse farmsteads typically found with a thatched, two-storey porch, like that at Lower Tor, near Poundsgate. Dartmoor's hard-wearing granite was also in demand further afield. The moorland quarries at Haytor, for example, provided stone for Nelson's Column, London Bridge, the Holborn Viaduct and New Scotland Yard in the capital. You can still see in the velvety, sheep-cropped grass the stone sets of the earliest horse-drawn tramway which took the stone down to Teignmouth for shipping.

Dartmoor's most notorious building, however, is the grim prison at Princetown, at the very heart of the moor. First constructed in 1806 for French and American prisoners of war, it became a criminal prison in 1850 and has remained so ever since.

Visitors started to come to Dartmoor and appreciate its wild, untamed beauty when the railway reached Exeter in 1844. Guides like James Perrott of Chagford led these early tourists out on to the moor and it was he who, in 1854, originated the custom of the Dartmoor letter boxes by leaving the tourists' visiting cards in a box at remote Cranmere Pool. Now there are about 500 such letter boxes scattered about the moor.

The Dartmoor National Park, set up in 1951, currently receives about eight million visits a year, and it has done a great deal towards improving visitor management and easing life for the 29,100 resident population by its system of special signposting of routes on the narrow, high-hedged lanes, and negotiating management agreements with farmers in ecologically important areas. About 40 per cent of the Park is common land, in which commoners have rights to graze under the Dartmoor Commons Act. Under the provisions of the Act, the Park authority now has joint responsibility for the commons, and public access is assured. Not so in the 15 per cent of the Park's area used by the Ministry of Defence. This is mainly in the northern

Terraced cottages at Ashburton, a convenient centre on the eastern edge of the moor

part of the moor and includes High Willhays (2,038ft/621m) and Yes Tor (2,030ft/618m), which form part of the huge Okehampton and Willsworthy Training Areas. The military has been training on Dartmoor since 1873, but conservationists were dismayed when, in 1991, the Duchy of Cornwall allowed the Army a further 21-year lease on its training area in the heart of the Park, despite the fact that such use is clearly incompatible with National Park purposes. The battle for Dartmoor's conservation is still not won.

The pinnacled tower of St Pancras, Widecombe-in-the-Moor, often known as 'the cathedral of the Moor'

EXMOOR

❦

Exmoor's most famous author, R D Blackmore, knew his homeland
well and his descriptive phrase 'the land lies softly', is an accurate
one. This is a gentle, pastoral landscape of rolling moorland,
deeply wooded valleys and rich farmland edged by tall hedges of
stunted beech. Where the land meets the sea, however, Exmoor has
a different face. Here, along the 30-mile (48km) stretch of
switchback coastline between Combe Martin and Minehead, is
some of the most spectacular and beautiful coastal scenery in
Britain, and it forms a dramatic highlight to one of the smallest and
most threatened of our National Parks.

Previous pages, the view from the roof of Exmoor, near the summit of Dunkery Beacon

The heather and gorse clad Brendon Hills form an eastern outlier of Exmoor

*E*xmoor has always attracted writers and artists, from Richard Doddridge Blackmore, author of the Victorian best-seller *Lorna Doone*, to Henry Williamson, whose natural history classic *Tarka the Otter* perhaps captures the essence of Exmoor better than anything which has been written before or since. Williamson wrote his famous tale of Tarka and White-Tip while living in a remote, 1s 6d-(7 ½ p)-a-week, cob-built cottage on the North Devon coast, and his description of the area from the book still takes some beating:

Exmoor is the high country of the winds, which are to the falcons and the hawks; clothed by whortleberry bushes and lichens and ferns and mossed trees in the goyals, which are to the foxes, the badgers, and the red deer; served by rain clouds and drained by rock-littered streams, which are to the otters.

The symbol of the Exmoor National Park authority, set up in 1954 to administer 268 square miles (694 sq km) of beautiful borderland between Devon and Somerset, is the majestic head of a ten-pointer red deer stag. This is Britain's largest animal and, outside Scotland, Exmoor has the largest wild herd. They are direct descendants of the wild deer which roamed the Exmoor forests in prehistoric times.

But Exmoor's red deer are also a major cause of controversy, with opinions deeply split between supporters of the traditional deer hunts, such as those carried out by the famous 'D and S,' the Devon and Somerset Staghounds which have a history going back to Saxon times, and those who find the whole idea of hunting barbaric. One thing is certain, the deer have to be culled to maintain a vigorous herd and the hunting, which has the support of most local farmers and their families, is carried out selectively and is largely sensitive to the deer's life-cycle. There is, for example, no hunting in the late spring and early summer when the calves, brilliantly camouflaged with their dappled coats that look like sunlight shining on dead leaves, are born.

Next to the red deer, Exmoor's most famous native residents are the hardy, shaggy-coated Exmoor ponies – a truly wild rare breed thought to be descended from the indigenous horses which survived the last Ice Age. These sturdy, agile creatures, not much bigger than a Shetland pony, have roamed Exmoor's moors and pastures for thousands of years and their wild, independent nature somehow encapsulates the spirit of Exmoor.

A simple memorial to R D Blackmore stands by the edge of Badgworthy Water, in the heart of Doone country

Where Exmoor Meets the Sea

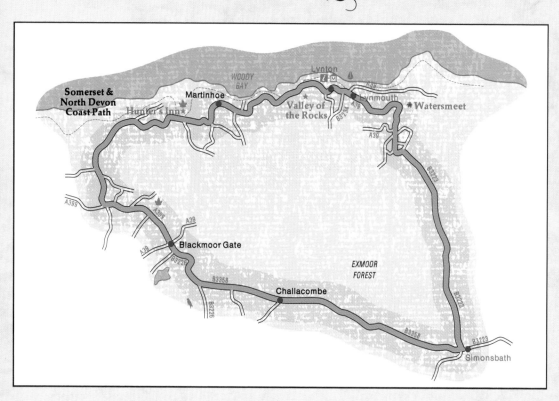

*T*his country drive, of about 31 miles (50km) explores the county boundary between Devon and Somerset, where Exmoor meets the sea. Steep, wooded combes plunge from the high plateau, creating shaded bays strewn with boulders. The scenery is spectacular, both along the coast and inland.

DIRECTIONS

Leave Lynton on the Lynmouth road and, on the descent, turn sharp left on to the B3234. Descend Lynmouth Hill (1 in 4) to Lynmouth. Here, turn right on to the A39 (sp. Barnstable) then reach Watersmeet. In ⅔ of a mile turn left on to the B3223 (sp. Simonsbath) and cross the river bridge. In ¾ mile, at the top of the ascent, turn sharp right to Simonsbath.

Here, turn right on to the B3358 (sp. Blackmoor Gate, Ilfracombe) for Challacombe. In 2⅓ miles, at the trunk road, turn right on to the A399 to Blackmoor Gate. Continue straight ahead on the A399 (sp. Combe Martin), then in 2 miles further, turn right, unclassified (sp. Trentishoe, Hunter's Inn). After 1¼ miles turn right, pass Holdstone car park on the left and in a further mile bear right (sp. Hunter's Inn).

At the Hunter's Inn turn left and ascend (sp. Martinhoe). In ¾ mile, at the top, turn left (sp. Woody Bay, Martinhoe). Pass Martinhoe church and in ½ mile branch left (sp. Woody Bay) then turn left and descend. Continue with signs Lynton, via Toll Road, past the Woody Bay Hotel. Go forward with the narrow coast road and in 1¾ miles, pass through the toll gate. In another mile, at the roundabout, go forward through the Valley of the Rocks and re-enter Lynton.

ON THE TOUR

Lynton

Set high on the cliff-top some 600 feet (200m) above Lynmouth, Lynton became a fashionable resort at the time of the Napoleonic Wars. It abounds in Victorian and Edwardian architecture, epitomised by the splendid town hall, built by the publisher George Newnes, who also sponsored the unusual water-powered cliff railway. The museum in St Vincent's Cottage, crammed with local interest, reflects the activities of the community. From the churchyard an orientation table identifies features on the Welsh coast. The church contains some exceptional marbles, but has been subjected to drab Victorian 'restoration'.

Lynmouth

The Victorians developed Lynmouth from a fishing village, building secluded gabled hotels and villas on the verdant hillsides, and eccentricities like the Rhenish Tower, on the quay, built to store saline bath water. Ferocious floods devastated the village in 1952; 90 houses were destroyed as the River Lyn burst its banks and swept through the sleeping village. Thirty-four people died, and a poignant exhibition records the fateful events in the Flood Memorial Hall.

The oldest area, around Mars Hill, is a medley of colour-washed cottages, and it was here that R D Blackmore stayed whilst researching *Lorna Doone*. Over the little footbridge, the pleasure gardens below the rising mass of Countisbury Hill afford a pleasant picnic area, with children's playground, bowls and a delightful grassy sward adjacent to the shingle beach.

Watersmeet

This aptly named National Trust beauty spot is located where the East Lyn River converges with Hoaroak Water, and cascades down a rocky ravine in a series of waterfalls. Watersmeet House, a fishing lodge built in 1832, offers refreshments during the summer.

Simonsbath

Note the beech hedges and herringbone walls established by John Knight in the 1820s. Access from the

The famous water powered cliff railway at Lynton

car park (signposted from the road) leads to a pleasantly landscaped picnic site, with local tourist information.

Hunter's Inn

At Hunter's Inn, set in mature woodland, a path continues to Heddon's Mouth, where the river rushes over smooth pebbles to the sea. For the energetic there is a climb to Heddon's Mouth Cleave, which leaves the path on the west of the river about halfway down. Relax with refreshments at Hunter's Inn afterwards – delightful gardens with ponds and greedy ducks.

Valley of the Rocks

Precarious rock formations pierce the skyline, and top the steep heather-clad hillocks standing sentinel between the sea and the moor; described by poet Robert Southey as 'rock reeling upon rock, stone piled upon stone, a huge terrifying reeling mass.'

A cynical commentator once dubbed Exmoor as 'ex-moor', and the truth is there is not much left of the original 'mountenous and cold ground much be Clouded with thick Foggs and Mists...overgrown with heath, and yielding but a pore kind of turf' which the Parliamentary Commissioners found in 1651. The 'Foggs and Mists' still regularly roll in from the Bristol Channel over the high points of The Chains and Dunkery Beacon, but piecemeal agricultural reclamation has reduced the 'hills of great height covered with heather' noted by Richard Jefferies in 1883, in the moorland heart of the National Park, so that they now cover about a quarter of the total area of the Park as opposed to a third. With luck, the greater power now available to the National Park authority under the Wildlife and Countryside Act of 1981 has stopped the worst of this attrition, although management agreements are still voluntary, and the Park authority has meagre resources with which to buy off the would-be 'improver'.

Having said that, the idea of making the landscape of Exmoor more productive in agricultural terms goes back to 1818 when a Midland ironmaster, John Knight, successfully bid for 15,000 acres (6075ha) of the former Royal Forest of Exmoor. Until then it had been used solely for hunting, with the exception of one not entirely successful attempt to grow oak trees to provide timber for the Navy.

During the next few decades John Knight and his son Frederic transformed the face of Exmoor by draining the waterlogged peats of the high ground, creating new farms and establishing the 'capital' of the forest at Simonsbath, and building the characteristic, beech-topped, earthen-banked hedges – such as the 29 mile (47km) example encircling Forest Wall – which are such a distinctive hallmark of Exmoor. John Knight's dream of growing arable crops on the heights, where the rainfall can be up to 60ins (152cm) a year, was never practical, but Frederic's system of root crop and grassland rotation is operated by some Exmoor farmers to this day. Knight also created one of the few stretches of open water in the National Park when he employed 200 Irish labourers in 1830 to build a dam across the headwaters of the River Barle, just beneath the boggy heights of The Chains near Challacombe. The result,

Lynton from Countisbury Common, on the North Devon Coast Path

Pinkworthy (pronounced Pinkery) Pond, is one of Exmoor's special wild places, now in the safe ownership of the National Park authority. Wimbleball Reservoir, a 370 acre (150ha) artificial lake created by the flooding of the Haddeo valley some 5 miles east of Dulverton, is of much more recent construction, but nevertheless very popular with sailors, anglers and picnickers.

Most holidaymakers explore Exmoor from the coastal resorts of Minehead, Ilfracombe, Lynton and Lynmouth. If, however, you want to see the real Exmoor, or what's left of it, you should base your exploration on the Knights' estate village of Simonsbath, the charming town of Dunster, or Dulverton – the modern 'capital' and the headquarters of the National Park authority, originally

Low tide in Lynmouth Harbour

Deepest Devon – high summer at Luccombe

built as a Poor Law institution. From here, it is easy to set out on foot for Williamson's 'high country of the winds' and to look down on the shimmering waters of the Bristol Channel with the dim blue outline of the South Wales coast on the horizon. There are over 600 miles (965km) of public footpaths and bridleways in the National Park, and the Park authority publishes an excellent series of waymarked walking guides and runs an extensive programme of guided walks.

You can reach the highest point of Dunkery Beacon (1,705ft/519m) quite easily as it is only half a mile (0.8km) across the moor from Dunkery Gate on the minor road between Wheddon

Cross and Luccombe. A longer and more pleasant walk can be taken by parking at Webber's Post, a mile south of Luccombe on the same road, then descending to East Water and crossing to ascend Cloutsham Ball. From Cloutsham, continue to Stoke Pero and go across Stoke Ridge to Dicky's Path, which returns with fine views across the Bristol Channel to Webber's Post along the northern edge of Dunkery.

Perhaps the finest walk in the whole of the National Park is that 30 mile (48km) stretch of the northern coastline which now forms part of the 600 mile (965km) South West Coast Path National Trail. It is here that the geology of Exmoor is revealed at a

glance, as the horizontal strata of the mainly Devonian rocks which form the backbone of the area are abruptly terminated by the crashing rollers of the sea. The rocks are mainly slates, grits and sandstones which were laid down as mud and sand up to 400 million years ago in the bed of a primeval ocean. Later earth movements threw them up into the position we see them in today.

The cliffs of the Exmoor coast rise up 1,200ft (366m) straight from the sea, making it the highest coastline in England. The sheltered north-facing cliffs, highest between The Foreland and Porlock Weir, still shelter extensive coastal woodlands which reach right down to the beach in the cleaves and coombes. This means that the birdwatcher can enjoy an unusual mixture of both woodland and sea birds, with woodpeckers and jays rubbing wings with fulmars, oystercatchers and even guillemots and razorbills at the western end of the coast. Here is the most dramatic part of the coastline, between the strange, rugged, dry Valley of the Rocks west of Lynton (thought to have originally been the course of the River Lyn) and Heddon's Mouth, where the River Heddon carves an impressively deep ravine down to the sea. The heavily wooded and thus appropriately named Woody Bay near Martinhoe is one of the scenic highspots of the coastal path, watched over by the

Watersmeet, where the fast-flowing waters of the East Lyn meet Farley Water and Hoaroak Water in a wooded cleave south of Lynton

No longer thought to be prehistoric, the clapper bridge of Tarr Steps over the River Barle is still a popular attraction

beetling cliffs of Wringapeak and Crock Point, while on Holdstone Down and the Great Hangman above Combe Martin Bay the heathland meets the sea, and the smell of the heather mingles with the salt sea tang.

Although Exmoor's land generally 'lies softly', it should never be underestimated – as illustrated by the disastrous floods in 1952 in Lynton and Lynmouth. Thirty people lost their lives after 9in (23cm) of rain fell on the heights of The Chains in 24 hours, turning the normally gentle River Lyn into a furious raging torrent. The results of that flood can still be seen today in the canalised river at Lynmouth and the huge delta which spreads out into the bay.

With an estimated three million day visitors a year, Exmoor is one of the least visited of our National Parks. This is hard to understand because its charms are endless and the variety of its scenery often spectacularly surprising. Too many of those who do come throng the summertime honeypots of Blackmore's 'Lorna Doone Country' in the Badgworthy valley south of Malmsmead and Oare – the scene of the tragically interrupted wedding of Lorna and John Ridd – or they clog the narrow approach road to the famous clapper bridge of Tarr Steps which crosses the River Barle west of Dulverton. For lovers of Exmoor's solitude, these are places to be avoided in the height of summer.

Blackmore himself wrote of his masterpiece: 'If I had dreamed that it would ever be more than a book of the moment, the descriptions of scenery – which I know as well as I know my garden – would have been kept nearer to their fact. I romanced herein, not to mislead any other, but solely for the uses of story.' That has not stopped generations of tourists following the Lorna Doone Trail, and it is a fact that many of the nefarious activities attributed to Carver Doone were based on the atrocities of a bandit family of the same name who lived in the remote valley in the mid-17th century.

Traditions have a habit of lingering long in the goyals and cleaves of Exmoor. When the English folk-song collector Cecil Sharp came to Porlock in the early years of this century he found the locals singing about a girl who had been captured and carried off by Danish sea-raiders. The incident of which they sang occurred in the year AD988.

Porlock Weir overlooks Porlock Bay, west of the village of Porlock itself

BRECON BEACONS

Seen from the valley of the River Usk to the north, the bold
escarpment of the Brecon Beacons has been likened to a petrified
tidal wave of red sandstone about to crash down on the
green-hedged, fertile valley beneath. That unspoken challenge has
attracted walkers and lovers of scenic beauty from all over Britain,
but the triple-topped central Beacons, with the ridge of the
Black Mountains to the east and the wild Black Mountain
to the west, have also long been a vital and highly valued
'lung' for the citizens of the industrial coal-mining towns of the
Welsh valleys.

Previous pages, Carreg Cennon in the Brecon Beacons, one of the most spectacular castle sites in Wales

The reigning peak of the Beacons, Pen y Fan, seen from the 'Roman Road' above the Upper Neuadd Reservoir

We had enjoyed an invigorating stroll from the village of Llanfrynach in the valley of the Usk up Cefn y Bryn, the easternmost of the five ridges which spread down north from the heights of the Brecon Beacons like the fingers of an outstretched hand. The views back down across the patchwork valley of the Usk had grown more and more extensive as we climbed and, looking west, we could see clearly the beckoning crests of the reigning summits of Cribyn and Pen y Fan across the intervening ridges. Our objective for the day had been the Cwm Oergwm Horseshoe, a semi-circular route taking in the easternmost Beacon of Gwaen Cerrig-llwydion and descending by the Cefn Cyff ridge back down to Llanfrynach and eventually back to Brecon. We gained the first top easily, enjoying the strange peat-hagged moonscape of Gwaen Cerrig-llwydion with its brown pools reflecting the early spring sun, and continued round the grey crags of Craig Cwarch which stood up like a cleric's collar round the rim of the cwm. When we reached Craig Cwm-

oergwm we descended slightly from the ridge, out of the biting April wind, to enjoy our packed lunch. We overlooked the glittering waters of the Upper Neuadd Reservoir in the valley far below, and the crags of Craig Fan-ddu frowned down on the opposite side of the head of the Fechan valley. Our leader turned to lead us off back down Cefn Cyff but, for four of us, the day was so good we informed him that we were going on to crest some of the other Beacons while we were there.

So we set off down the grassy slopes to the col of Craig Cwm Cynwyn, where the so-called Roman Road (which may have linked a camp at Penydarren, near Merthyr Tydfil, with the Roman fort of Y Gaer 2 miles (3.2km) west of Brecon) crosses the Brecons ridge in a cutting 1961ft (598m) above the sea. A short, stiff climb took us up to Cribyn, at 2608ft (795m) the third highest of the Beacons, and into the teeth of a gale which made it difficult to stand on the exposed summit. The view we obtained was well worth it, however. Across the yawning gap of Cwm Sere the precipices of table-topped Pen y

Fan (2906ft/886m) stood out clearly, the horizontal bands of rose-red sandstone and shale and green bands of vegetation glowing in the strengthening sun. Behind, the hooded shape of Corn Du peeped over the shoulder of Pen y Fan. It was a perfect picture of mountain majesty, and as we descended the steep ridge of Bryn-teg, accompanied by gliders soaring effortlessly on the thermals across the face of Pen y Fan, we were sorry our companions were not with us to enjoy it. Attractive as the Beacons are with their easily obtainable summits – the day before we had topped Pen y Fan and back in half a day – they should never be underestimated. A simple stone obelisk on Craig Cwm-llwch, just below the summit of Corn Du and above the perfect little glacial tarn of Llyn-cwm-llwch, serves as a reminder of the dangers of these apparently gentle hills. It commemorates little Tommy Jones, a five-year-old miner's son from Maerdy in the Rhondda, who disappeared in 1900 during a short walk from the last farm in the valley; his body was not found for a month. Almost every year tough SAS

Two miles west of Brecon are the foundations of the Roman fort of Y Gaer

commandos from the nearby Sennybridge Camp lose their way, and sometimes their lives, in these deceptive mountains. The moral is, if you are walking in the Brecon Beacons, go prepared.

The Brecon Beacons National Park, founded in 1957, covers 522 square miles (1,357 sq km), and the central Beacons are the main attraction for most visitors. On either side of the Beacons are two sharply contrasting ranges of hills with confusingly similar names.

The Black Mountains (plural) to the east are a roughly north–south range of sandstone hills between Hay-on-Wye in the north and Abergavenny in the south. Split by deep valleys known as darrens, they are watched over by the summits of Hay Bluff and Abergavenny's twin guardians, the distinctive Sugar Loaf and Skirrid Fawr. The Black Mountains lie on the border between Wales and England, and Offa's Dyke, the boundary between the two countries constructed by King Offa of Mercia in the 8th century, still marches along their eastern crest. It now carries the Offa's Dyke National Trail. Below the hills to the west lies Llangorse Lake (Lyn Syfaddan), the largest natural lake in

Capel-y-ffin in the Vale of Ewyas, in the Black Mountains – the name means 'the chapel on the bundary'

the National Park and noted for its interesting birdlife.

Beyond the Beacons and across the great expanse of wild moorland summits and deep wooded valleys which formed the ancient royal hunting forest of Fforest Fawr, lie the even wilder western summits of the Black Mountain (Mynydd Du),

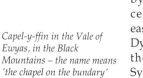

formerly known as the Carmarthen Fan. These great sweeping escarpments in many ways match those of the central Beacons, but this is much wilder and less often visited country – a place where myths and legends abound like the frequent mists which cloak the glaciated heights. One of my favourite stories is that of the fairy princess of Llyn y Fan fach, the wind-whipped lake which lies at the foot of the sweeping precipices of Bannau Sir Gaer above Llanddeusant. The story is that the princess emerged from the lake to seduce and eventually marry a poor young shepherd boy from the hamlet of Myddfai in the valley below. Her dowry was as many fairy sheep,

Snow dusts the north-facing scarp of the Black Mountain, near Llanddeusant

A Walk to Llyn-Cwm-Llwch

*A*lthough bleak and forbidding on dull, wet days, the massive plateau of the Brecon Beacons is transformed by fine weather into a region of inspiring beauty. The walk is approximately 6½ miles (10.5km) long, and climbs from the valley of the Afon Tarell to Llyn-cwm-llwch, an isolated glacial tarn at the foot of Cwm-llwch. The scenery is dramatic, making an imposing setting for the wildlife of the Brecon Beacons. Although the walk is generally easy and does not tackle the peaks, it is steep in parts, encompassing a wide range of habitats, and goes right into the heart of the Beacons. From the valley bottoms, the mountains may

look more like hills. Do not be deceived, however, because they can be as testing as any in Britain. Stout, waterproof footwear is essential as well as sensible clothing.

DIRECTIONS

1 Cross the A470 and go over a stile. Cross the field to another stile and turn left on to a minor road. At a T-junction, turn right and then left after a short distance. Ignore a turning to the left, and turn right and immediately left when you reach a junction.

Along the narrow lanes look out for ferns such as polypody, male fern and

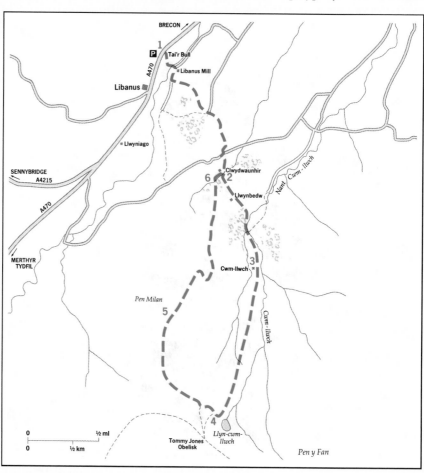

bracken, as well as flowers including red campion and foxgloves growing in the hedgerow. In the spring, butterflies such as green-veined whites and small tortoiseshells visit the flowers to feed. Hedgerow shrubs include hawthorn and blackthorn, their berries providing food in the autumn for birds.

2 Pass through a gate at Clwydwaunhir. Walk past the house, cross the stream on your left using stepping stones, and go over a stile. Continue across the fields, crossing two more stiles, until you reach the buildings at Llwynbedw. Continue heading south over two further stiles, then keep the open woodland on your right.

Check for woodland birds: chaffinches and several species of tit may be present throughout the year, joined by warblers in summer.

Bear to the right when you reach a river and continue through some woodland and over a footbridge.

Streams in the Brecon Beacons provide a good habitat for brown trout, which generally remain small in size. The comparatively clean air in this part of the Beacons allows abundant mosses and pollution-sensitive lichens to grow on the trunks and branches of the trees.

3 When you reach Cwm-llwch, follow the signposted detour around the building. Beyond this, return to the main track, cross two stiles and continue up the hill. Cross the hill fence at the National Trust signpost, and pass two cairns. Ignore the left-hand fork in the track and continue heading towards Cwm-llwch.

Look out for rowan or mountain ash trees. They produce bright red berries in the late summer and autumn – food for ring-ouzels before they begin their migration south, and for redwings and fieldfares, which winter in Britain.

4 At Llyn-cwm-llwch, pause to admire the glacial tarn set against the backdrop of Craig Cwm-llwch. The lake has a small population of palmate newts, and aquatic vegetation grows around its margins.

Llyn-cwm-Llwch lies like a jewel at the heart of the Beacons

If time permits, a detour can be made to the Tommy Jones obelisk via a track to the left. This commemorates the death of a small boy in 1900.

Return to the original path and walk north-west around the valley head.

The open, grassy moorland is home to meadow pipits. These rather nondescript brown birds have a thin call and a distinctive song-flight in the breeding season. They sometimes fall victim to merlins, which occasionally pass through the area. Wheatears are summer visitors to the Brecon Beacons and scold humans intruding into their territories with loud, clacking calls. Look out for buzzards overhead. They have broad, rounded wings and utter a mewing call in flight.

5 Just before you reach Pen Milan the path becomes broader and soon passes between two banks. The path bends sharply right then left as it descends. Continue down the hill, walking between the two banks.

The vegetation in many parts of the Beacons has been reduced to acid grassland for sheep grazing, and mat-grass is a characteristic species. Listen for skylarks singing in flight, and look for fox droppings deposited in prominent places. Sensitive noses may also detect their pungent scent.

6 Go through a ford, then through a gate to the right at the bottom of the hill. Carry on to Clwydwaunhir, then retrace your steps to the start of the walk.

Geology and glacial features

Much of the Brecon Beacons range is composed of Old Red Sandstone. This sedimentary rock was laid down by slow-flowing rivers, then folded and raised by earth movements to form the plateau we see today. The last Ice Age, which in geological terms, ended comparatively recently – 10,000 years ago – has left plenty of signs of its passing in the Beacons, several of which can be seen on this walk. Cwm-llwch is a glacial cirque – a natural amphitheatre carved by the erosion of ice and frozen snow, assisted by the shattering action of alternate freezing and thawing. A small glacier – long since gone – formed on its slopes and at what was once its base lies Llyn-cwm-llwch. Around the northern shores of the lake are small moraines – the remains of rock fragments carved by the glacier.

Picard's Tower, at Tretower Castle, near Crickhowell, is a 13th-century round keep built within the remains of an earlier tower

cattle, goats and horses as he could count in a single breath as they emerged from the lake. But there was one drawback: if he was moved to strike her three times she would return to the lake taking her dowry with her. Over the years the inevitable happened, a touch here and a touch there, and finally he tapped her lightly on the arm for laughing at a funeral. The fairy prophecy was fulfilled, and the princess returned to the lake taking her cattle with her. But she had left the shepherd with three fine sons who, having learned the gift of healing from their mother, became the fabled Physicians of Myddfai and the most famous doctors in the whole of the Principality.

South of the mountain masses of the Beacons lies another, quite different landscape of fretted white limestone pavements, secret wooded valleys and spectacular caves and waterfalls. Again geology provides the answer, as a belt of carboniferous limestone and millstone grit runs across the southern edge of the National Park to create this entirely unexpected scenic surprise. The best place to see it is near Ystradfellte, where the Rivers Mellte and Hepste play hide-and-seek over steps of grit and limestone and where, at Porth yr Ogof, the Mellte disappears completely into the huge, yawning maw of one of the biggest cave systems in Britain. Further downstream a series of waterfalls marks where the river reaches the gritstone. The names of the waterfalls are as delightful as their sylvan settings – Sgwd Clun-gwyn (White Meadow

Fall), Sgwd y Pannwr (Fall of the Fuller) on the Mellte, and Sgwd yr Eira (Fall of Snow) on the Hepste, where you can actually walk behind the fall on an eroded ledge of rock.

The Upper Tawe valley, to the west, is the place for the non-caving tourist to explore the subterranean splendours of the Beacons' limestone belt. The Dan yr Ogof cave system is open to the public as a show cave, and is well worth a visit if only to see the spectacular Cathedral Cavern – over 150ft (46m) long and 70ft (21m) high. Conveniently near by is the National Park's 40 acre (16ha) Craig-y-nos Country Park which occupies the 'pleasure grounds' of Craig-y-nos Castle, the former home of the popular Victorian opera singer, Madame Adelina Patti.

The human history of the Brecon Beacons begins long before the Romans marched this way. A group of stone circles has been identified on the western side of Fforest Fawr, and a score of Iron Age hillforts, once occupied by the Silures (who gave their name to one of the oldest rock types found in the area) are found in the National Park. The most impressive are Carn Goch, near

Llanthony Priory, in the Vale of Ewyas – the romantic remains of a 12th-century Augustinian foundation

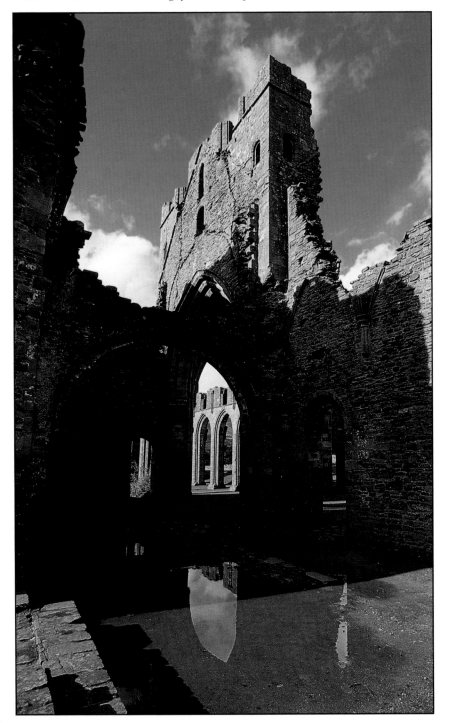

A distant view of the Black Mountains from the boulder-strewn bed of the River Usk

Llangadog on the slopes of the Black Mountain, and Castell Dinas at the head of the Rhiangoll valley. The remains of a prehistoric crannog, or man-made island, have been identified in Llangorse Lake. Long after the Romans had subdued the Silures with their extensive system of roadways which centred on the fort of Yr Gaer, near Brecon, an obscure but powerful Dark Age Irish prince known as Brychan gave his name to the whole area (in Welsh, *Brycheiniog*). After the

Norman Conquest a string of fine stone-built castles was constructed on the eastern side of the Park, mainly along the valleys of the Usk and Honddu. The finest surviving examples are probably those of Hay, Brecon (now a hotel), Trecastle, Tretower and Crickhowell.

Carreg Cennen, perched like a rotting tooth on a 300ft (92m) limestone crag at the foothills of the Black Mountain near Llandeilo, is one of the most spectacular castle sites in this land of castles. During its 800-year history it has suffered a chequered career of being held, retaken and held again by the Welsh and the English, and is always worth a visit. Children love the 230ft (70m) vaulted passageway cut into the living rock of the crag which leads to a natural cave that may have served as a dungeon.

The charming – mainly Georgian – township of Brecon (population 7,200) is the focal point of the National Park and the home of the National Park authority. Situated at the confluence of the Rivers Usk and Honddu at the foot of the northern scarp of the Beacons, it is an ideal centre for the exploration of the National Park. There is a county museum, the cathedral church of St John, and markets on Tuesdays and Fridays. The National Park authority has an information centre here and runs a very good Brecon Beacons Mountain Centre just off the A470 near Libanus on the edge of the Mynydd Illtud Common. This is worth a visit before you embark on a walking expedition in the Beacons, or explore any other part of the National Park.

One of the earliest tourists to visit the area was the cynical journalist Daniel Defoe, who arrived in 1724. The mountains filled him with horror. Equating them with the Alps or the Andes, Defoe wrote: 'Sometimes we see these mountains rising up at once, from the lower valleys, to the highest summits which makes the height look horrid and frightful, even worse than those mountains abroad…'

Tastes in the appreciation of scenery have changed, and to today's visitor the sudden sight of those beckoning Beacons is a source of inspiration rather than trepidation.

The essence of the Beacons – the view from Mynydd Llangattock across the valley of the Usk towards the distant Black Mountains

PEMBROKESHIRE COAST

Pembrokeshire, sometimes known as 'Little England Beyond Wales', has held a fascination for English visitors ever since the first Norman warlords forced their way in 800 years ago, leaving a string of 50 fine castles in their wake. To the Welsh, the Pembrokeshire Coast has been known since the 11th century as *Gwlad hud a lledrith* – the land of magic and enchantment – and its 230 miles (368km) of rugged cliffs, inviting sandy beaches and enormous, raucous, seabird colonies still retain that magic for today's visitor.

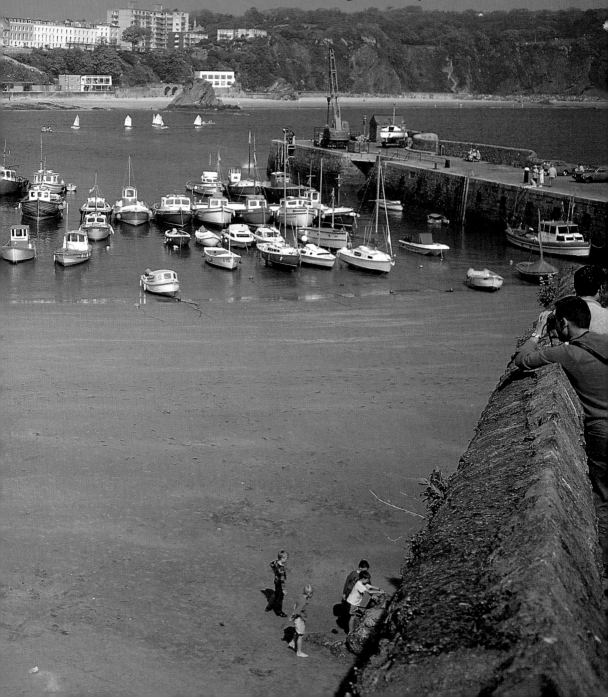

The great glory of Pembrokeshire is its rugged coastline, seen here near Manorbier

Previous pages, the harbour at Tenby, the Park's largest town

The anonymous author of *The Mabinogion*, an 11th-century collection of Welsh folk legends, started it all. His description of the old Celtic kingdom of Dyfed (which later became Pembrokeshire but has now reverted to its original name) as 'the land of magic and enchantment' was perhaps the earliest written attempt to sum up the outstanding natural beauty of this wonderful westernmost outpost of Wales.

His search for appropriate superlatives was followed a century later by a Pembrokeshire-born Welshman of Norman stock, Giraldus Cambrensis (Gerald the Welshman). Born in the romantically sited Manorbier Castle, overlooking the fine beaches of Manorbier Bay, Giraldus had no hesitation in dubbing his birthplace 'the most delectable spot in Wales', and few of today's holiday-makers would disagree. The well-preserved battlemented towers of the 12th-century castle have the authority of one of the great Crusader castles of the Middle East, and the bay beneath its walls has more than a touch of Mediterranean beauty.

Giraldus's *Itinerary Through Wales*, written in 1188 as he travelled round to enlist recruits for the Crusades, gives a vivid picture of life as it was in the late 12th century. 'Penbroch' (Pembroke), declared Giraldus with perhaps understandable loyalty, was '...the finest part of the Province of Demetia

The best time, however, to see Pembrokeshire's glorious wildflowers is in the spring or early summer, when the cliff tops are ablaze with colour. The equable climate allows plants like pink thrift, sunshine yellow kidney vetch and gorse, yellow cowslip and primrose, scarlet campion and misty bluebell to flower almost continuously from the end of February onwards through the spring. One of the greatest joys of the Pembrokeshire Coast National Park is to walk along part of the roller-coaster 170 mile (272km) Pembrokeshire Coast Path National Trail at this time of the year, before the summer season crowds arrive and while the flowers are still at their best.

Stack Rocks, otherwise known as the Elegug Stacks, off the Catlemartin peninsula, are home to thousands of razorbills and guillemots

(Dyfed). And Demetia is the most beautiful part of Wales.' The 13 million annual visitors to the 225 square mile (583 sq km) Pembrokeshire Coast National Park, set up in 1952, seem to bear out Giraldus's extravagant claim.

The Pembrokeshire Coast is the warmest British National Park, and Dale, on the St Ann's Head peninsula, the sunniest place in all Wales. The climate, with a mean minimum temperature of 40°F (4°C), is similar to that of the Channel Islands. This allows the National Park authority, uniquely among its British counterparts, to run guided walks to see wildflowers during the Christmas holiday!

To stroll along the crest of these beetling cliffs, with the salty tang of the sea mingling with the scents of the endless carpet of wildflowers, and the only sound the crashing of the Atlantic breakers and the harsh cries of the razorbills, guillemots and kittiwakes, is an unforgettable experience which draws walkers and lovers of the best of British coastal scenery back time and again to this delectable spot.

The off-shore islands of the Pembrokeshire Coast – Caldey, Skomer, Skokholm, Grassholm, Ramsey and Gateholm – were all given their names by Viking sea-raiders, *holm* meaning a small island and *oy* or *ey* a larger one. The islands are famous among nature lovers for their huge, protected colonies of seabirds, particularly Skomer and Skokholm's Manx shearwaters and Grassholm's gannets, two of the largest colonies of these birds in Britain.

Each island has its own highly individual character and devotees. Caldey, the only one permanently inhabited, is perhaps best-known for its Cistercian abbey, where the white-robed monks till the fertile soil and manufacture sweet-smelling Caldey Island perfume. It is reached by boat trips which operate regularly from the popular holiday centre of Tenby.

Similar trips from Dale, Marloes and Solva take boatloads of binocular-armed birdwatchers on the short trip to Skomer, a National Nature Reserve covering 722 acres (292ha) and the site of one of the finest seabird colonies in Europe. Here large colonies of fulmar, kittiwake, guillemot, and the dumpy, penguin-like symbol of the National Park, the razorbill, nest on the steep seacliffs which can be

Marloes Sands from Red Cliff, on the spectacular Pembrokeshire Coast Path

reached by a convenient self-guided nature trail.

Everywhere you look in the shallow soil of Skomer you will see the breeding burrows of two other bird species for which the island is famous. One is the comical, clown-like puffin which nests underground here, but the real Skomer speciality is the mysterious Manx shearwater, and over 100,000 of these nocturnal wanderers

of the sea breed here in these shallow burrows, only emerging under the cover of darkness.

There is another large colony of shearwaters on Skokholm, the site of the first bird observatory in Britain. It was established in 1933 by the famous Pembrokeshire naturalist, Richard Lockley, who lived here in idyllic seclusion from 1927 to 1939. Storm petrels, known to sailors as 'Mother Carey's Chickens', also breed here alongside the mercurial, red-beaked chough – black-cloaked master of the seacliff thermals.

The other islands of Grassholm, Ramsey and Gateholm are not usually visited by the public, although some boat trips take visitors out to see them at closer quarters. Viewed from the mainland in early summer, Grassholm often seems to have a white halo, or

The tiny harbour of Porthgain, on St David's Head

Wild Flowers

Sea Sandwort
A common sight along
Britain's shoreline, sea
sandwort (Honkenya
peploides) is a pale yellowy-
green plant, recognisable by
its very fleshy, oval, pointed
leaves. It grows in tightly-
packed carpets along sandy
or pebbly beaches, and may
easily be first mistaken for
a sea-washed tide-line.

For centuries children have made daisy chains, held buttercups under each other's chins and blown dandelion clocks to tell the time. Today wild flowers are still all around us, a link with the natural world along the road verges, on the building sites, along the ever-diminishing margins of our fields. The appeal and variety of wild flowers in Britain is enormous, and during the summer parts of the coast practically glow with them.

The coastal flora is one of the particular delights of Pembrokeshire – where the narrow lanes weave between steep banks and walls, placing these colourful beauties at eye level. Coastal heathland is one of the most attractive habitats in Britain but, sadly, also one of the most vulnerable. Many areas have disappeared through changes in land use; others have simply been degraded. Even today, the remaining examples are not entirely secure, even when managed by such a responsible body as the National Trust. These heaths are often in dramatic settings, as is the case with the Pembrokeshire Coast National Park, and they can attract large numbers of visitors. Accidental and

Bell Heather
Often confused with the
heather which covers so
much of Britain's uplands,
purple-flowering bell
heather (Erica cinera) is not
actually a true heather.
While sometimes found on
sandy heathland, on high
moorland its presence is
an indication of areas of
drier ground.

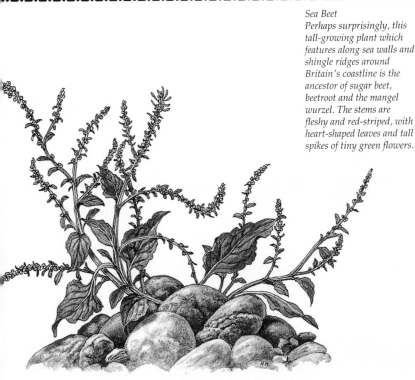

Sea Beet
Perhaps surprisingly, this tall-growing plant which features along sea walls and shingle ridges around Britain's coastline is the ancestor of sugar beet, beetroot and the mangel wurzel. The stems are fleshy and red-striped, with heart-shaped leaves and tall spikes of tiny green flowers.

deliberate fires are always a threat, as is erosion by trampling. However, if visitors keep strictly to well-worn and designated paths the adverse effects of this can be kept to a minimum.

Spring and early summer are the best months to visit Pembrokeshire for the flowers: deep purple clumps of bell-heather contrast with paler sprays of ling and the bright yellow flowers of gorse. It is not only humans that find this display attractive: insects in abundance feed on the nectar, and bumble bees and butterflies are particularly in evidence. Look out, too, for birds such as wheatears, stonechats and whitethroats.

When walking near the coast here, look out for wild flowers such as sea beet, mallow, toadflax and red campion. On more exposed banks you may see gorse, sea campion, thrift and sea carrot. On the heathland itself, in addition to the dominant species of

dwarf gorse, bell heather and ling, look for harebell, sawwort, thrift and tormentil. Wood sage and fleabane may be spotted among the gorse and heathers, and species such as herb Robert and navelwort in stony crevices and walls.

You should note that it is illegal to uproot any wild plant without the landowner's permission and more than 60 species are further protected from picking, sale or collection of seed. These most vulnerable species include many of our orchids, as well as other less showy flowers. The best policy is not to pick any wild flowers.

True to the old saying, Britain's three species of gorse flower at different times through the year, ensuring that kissing is always in season.

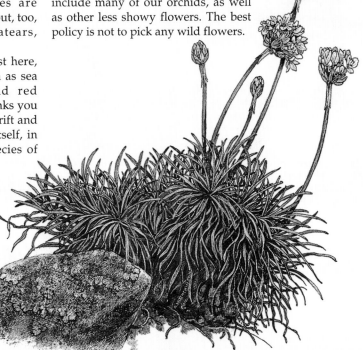

Thrift
The breeze-blown pink flower-heads of thrift (Armeria maritima) are a familiar sight along the sea-cliffs of Britain's coastline, bobbing above their cushion of coarse, grass-like leaves. Thrift flowers from late spring to early autumn, but is seen at its best around the height of summer.

The Green Bridge of Wales, a famous sea-eroded arch off the Castlemartin peninsula

even a snow-capped summit. This is the massive gannetry of Grassholm; with over 20,000 birds it is one of the largest in Britain. They seem to have driven out a sizeable puffin colony which once also existed here, but kittiwake, razorbill, guillemot and great black-backed gulls still nest alongside the ruling gannets. Boats also cross the treacherous waters of the Ramsey Sound to see the autumn breeding grounds of the grey seal colony on Ramsey Island.

Pembrokeshire's greatest glory is its coastline, and because nowhere in the National Park is more than ten miles (16km) from the sea – and most places are only 3 miles (4.8km) away – many visitors never stray from the narrow confines of beach, bay and cliff. In doing so, they miss some of the Park's hidden attractions; the secret, inner

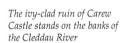

Haverfordwest where the National Park has its headquarters. This is a landscape of mudflats, reedbeds and woodlands, where small communities like Llangwm, Lawrenny, castle-crowned Carew and Picton Ferry dip their toes in the tidal waters leading south to the broad, natural harbour of Milford Haven. The heavily industrialised areas of Pembroke Dock and Milford Haven itself were excluded by the Park boundary, and the huge oil refineries and their associated silver storage tanks and giant supertankers plying in and out of the estuary bear evidence to the wisdom of that far-sighted decision by the National Park Commissioners 40 years ago.

The north-western corner of the National Park, where the Ordovician rocks of the Presely Hills rear up to their high point of Foel Cwm Cerwyn (1760ft/536m), were well known to prehistoric man. Burial cairns, burial chambers, hillforts and stone circles litter the smooth, rounded slopes covered in heather and gorse and now grazed by sheep. On a clear day the views from their rugged, rock-strewn summits extend south as far as Dunkery Beacon on Exmoor across the Bristol Channel, to Cadair Idris in Snowdonia to the north, and to the Wicklow Hills in Ireland across to the west.

Perhaps the Presely Hills greatest claim to fame came when archaeologists proved them to be the source of the fabled blue stones which form the inner circle of the

The ivy-clad ruin of Carew Castle stands on the banks of the Cleddau River

sanctuary of the wooded, winding estuaries of the Daugleddau between Pembroke and Haverfordwest, and the isolated moorland block of the Presely Hills in the north.

The Daugleddau is the name given to the drowned estuaries, or rias, of the Western and Eastern Cleddau, the Carew and the Cresswell rivers which eat deeply into the heart of the land, almost reaching the county town of

most celebrated prehistoric monument in Britain – Stonehenge on far-off Salisbury Plain. Many theories have been postulated as to how Neolithic man managed to get the 80 massive stones of spotted dolerite to Wiltshire, 180 miles (288km) away, but most experts now believe they were rafted using rivers and the sea, and then rolled across country for the final lap. However it was achieved, it was undoubtedly a massive feat of civil engineering by an apparently primitive people.

One of the most striking prehistoric monuments in Wales, let alone Pembrokeshire, is the extraordinary 7ft (2.1m) high Neolithic chambered long barrow of Pentre Ifan on the northern slopes of the Presely Hills, 4 miles

The Neolithic chambered long barrow of Pentre Ifan, near Newport

(6.4km) south-east of Newport. The capstone of Pentre Ifan is 16½ ft (5m) long, thought to weigh 17 tons, and is supported by three massive uprights. Actually the denuded remains of a barrow once covered by earth, it always reminds me of a milking stool waiting to be used by a giantess. Carreg Samson, at Longhouse near Abercastle, is another splendid monument in an impressive setting overlooking the blue waters of the bay.

Everywhere you look on the Pembrokeshire Coast there is evidence of history. Promontories are bounded

by the embankments of Iron Age hillforts (here known by the Irish word *rath*, showing the strong links across the Irish Sea), and the tiny, walled medieval 'city' of St David's, with its lilac-pink cathedral and Bishop's Palace, is one of Wales's most sacred spots.

Another magical place on these rocky shores where the light of Christianity first shone is the tiny chapel of St Govan, nestling at the foot of the cliffs near Bosherston. A steep climb down narrow steps brings you to a hermitage which may date from the 5th century, and it is hard to imagine a more remote spot for a holy man's devotions. Access to St Govan's Chapel is sometimes restricted because of the unwelcome presence of the NATO Castlemartin Artillery Ranges which extend along one of the finest stretches of the coast between here and Linney Head. More than 5,800 acres (2,347 ha) of the National Park are still used in this way, and the public is excluded when notices are posted and the red flags are flying – proof that even in this apparently unspoiled area of wild, natural scenery compromises are still being made.

Bosherston Lily Pools, artificial lakes formed by the blocking of three streams, are now a National Nature Reserve

SNOWDONIA

Seen on a satellite photograph, Snowdonia somewhat resembles a
knot of sinewy muscles clenched on the shoulder of Wales. Here is
the highest land south of the Border, an uncompromising landscape of rugged, rocky mountains whose ridges and summits are
as wild and as challenging as any in Britain. But there is another,
gentler side to Snowdonia, one of beautiful wooded glens with
spectacular tumbling waterfalls, friendly blue-slate villages where
Welsh is still the first language, and some of the finest unspoilt
beaches in Wales.

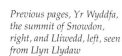

Previous pages, Yr Wyddfa, the summit of Snowdon, right, and Lliwedd, left, seen from Llyn Llydaw

The rocky peak of Tryfan, seen from Llyn Idwal

Despite the frequent drenching showers of autumnal rain, it was hot work traversing the boulder-strewn, heathery terrace which cut diagonally up the mountain. We were on Tryfan, the 3,010ft (917m) fang of naked rock which towers above the A5 Holyhead road as it approaches Ogwen Cottage in the heart of the Snowdonia National Park. Seen from the road, Tryfan appears to be inaccessible, although generations of coach travellers have been fooled by the figures of Adam and Eve, the two natural 10ft (3m) high monoliths which stand side by side on the summit. Tryfan was perfectly described in 1778 by Thomas Pennant as he looked down from the neighbouring height of Glyder Fach, our eventual objective of the day: 'In the midst of the vale far below rises the singular mountain Trevaen, assuming on this side a pyramidal form, naked and very rugged'. Rugged is certainly the right adjective to describe Tryfan, reputed to be the only one of the 14 Welsh 3,000-footers which cannot be climbed without the use of hands. It is also the nearest major summit to a main road, but although the rocky crest is a mere half-

mile from the A5 as the raven soars, it is still a good 2,000 vertical feet (610m) above it – hence our rather sweaty condition as we rounded a rocky corner on the aptly named Heather Terrace to emerge, thankfully, on to level ground. It was my friend Pete, a former leader of the Snowdonia Mountain Rescue Team, who first noticed that our strenuous exertions were being watched. 'Look over there', he exclaimed, pointing ahead of us on the Terrace. 'He'll show you how to do it.'

There, standing knee-deep in the heather and looking very imperious

was the biggest billy goat I've ever seen. His shaggy white coat had black patches and his long flowing beard reached down to brush the tops of the heather. On his proud head was a magnificent set of sweeping horns which would not have disgraced an Alpine ibex. Having dismissed our feeble efforts at climbing, this wonderful monarch of the hills casually stepped off the edge of the Terrace and plunged vertically and perfectly safely down the terrifyingly steep east face of the mountain, to rejoin his harem of nannies which we could now just make out grazing peacefully on the lower slopes of Cwm Tryfan, 1,500ft (457m) below. The herd of wild goats on Tryfan is well known among the climbers who scramble on this popular peak, but they are more often talked about than seen, and we were indeed lucky to have had such a close encounter with their bearded patriarch.

There are similar small, elusive herds of wild goats on the equally rugged slopes of the Rhionogs and the Moelwyns. All are thought to be descended from the original wild goats of Snowdonia which played such a big part in clearing the slopes of their virgin tree cover.

Before the ubiquitous sheep was introduced, goats and cattle were the chief source of income for Snowdonia's hill farmers from medieval times. They are mentioned by Shakespeare in *Henry V*, when Pistol swears he would not eat Fluellen's leek, 'for Cadwallader and all his goats!' Modern farmers, who

On the Precipice Walk, Dolgellau, looking across the valley of the Mawddach

Looking down the Ogwen Falls, near Ogwen Cottage

still regard the goats with proprietorial pride, value them because they graze in the most inaccessible places, thus dissuading incautious, less nimble sheep from straying on to perilous ledges and possibly getting crag-fast or falling to their deaths.

The chief industry of the 827 square mile (2,142 sq km) Snowdonia National Park, set up in 1951 and the second largest after the Lake District, is still hill farming although tourism, as elsewhere, is becoming increasingly important to the local economy. But in Snowdonia, above all the other National Parks, the fires of an ever-present, proud nationalism, perhaps best defined in the Welsh word *hwyl*, still burn as fiercely as they did in Shakespeare's or even Henry V's day. There is still an understandable resentment over things such as outsiders owning second homes here and the impositions, particularly in planning matters, that National Park status sometimes inflicts on local people. Seventy per cent of the resident population of 23,800 people regard Welsh as their mother tongue, and the visitor will notice that road and footpath signs are always given in Welsh first. Don't be confused if you can't find the place regularly signposted Llwybr Cyhoeddus, on the

map, it simply indicates the start of one of Snowdonia's public footpaths and rights of way which total 2,175 miles (3,480km). Walking and climbing in the hills is the most popular pursuit for Snowdonia's 11 million annual visitors, and hills like Tryfan were one of the birthplaces of the modern sport of rock-climbing. Milestone Buttress, one of the most popular climbs on Tryfan, was first climbed by O G Jones as early as 1899.

The landscape of Snowdonia's three major mountain ranges has graphically been described as an arrow and a star. The shaft and flight feathers of the arrow is the ridge of the Carneddau, the largest mass of high ground in Wales with six summits over 3,000ft (914m), topped by Carnedd Llewelyn

Llyn Idwal fills the glacial cirque of Cwm Idwal, in this view towards the sunlit rocks of Idwal Slabs

(3,484ft/1,061m) and Carnedd Dafydd (3,426ft/1,044m) which are named after two of the last Welsh princes. This high, semi-arctic wilderness is bordered to the north by the sea, to the east by the River Conwy and to the south by the line of Thomas Telford's 1815 Holyhead road which crosses the Nant Ffrancon pass under Tryfan by Ogwen Cottage.

The sharply-pointed arrow head is formed by the weird, frost-splintered plateau of the Glyders, accurately described by Charles Kingsley in 1857 as 'that enormous desolation, the dead bones of the eldest born of time', and topped by Glyder Fawr (3,279ft/999m) and Glyder Fach (3,262ft/994m).

That rocky arrowhead, which includes Tryfan, points unerringly at the 'star' of the central Snowdon massif, across the deep glaciated cleft of the Llanberis Pass, now threaded by the A4086 Capel Curig-to-Llanberis road. Although the name Snowdon is now usually taken to refer to the 3,560ft (1,085m) summit of the massif, its actual name in Welsh is Yr Wyddfa, which means the great tumulus. It gets its English name from passing sailors who noted that the high hills of North Wales were often covered in snow, and named them *Snawdun*, or *Snaudune* on early maps. Llewelyn the Great, remembered in Carnedd Llewelyn,

styled himself 'Princeps Aberfaw Dominus Snawdon' in 1230, and the name Snowdonia has been in use ever since.

In former times, the whole of the mountainous region around the Snowdon summit was known as Eryri, which has been translated as the abode of eagles. Although, sadly, these majestic, broad-winged birds no longer soar across the crags of Snowdon it is easy to imagine them doing so, and with luck they might return one day.

Yr Wyddfa stands at the point of this star of radiating ridges, most of which are now crossed by well-worn paths. It has been estimated that on a typical summer Sunday as many as 1,500 walkers reach Snowdon's summit, and about 1,000 more are carried up by the famous rack-and-pinion railway from Llanberis, which opened in 1896. Snowdon summit has been described by none other than the Prince of Wales as 'the highest slum in Europe', and the crowds, litter and café at the top do sometimes seem more appropriate to a run-down seaside resort.

But if you choose to walk up Snowdon in the off-season by one of the popular routes, such as the Miners' Track or the Pyg Track from Pen-y-Pass at the summit of the Llanberis Pass, you will be amazed at the untamed wildness of the scene,

Below, elderflowers adorn the bridge over the River Glaslyn, Beddgelert

Right, Harlech Castle commands fine views towards the peaks of Snowdonia to the north

The power of Snowdonia's rivers is well illustrated in this view of Pont-y-Pair Bridge, Betwys y Coed

rapids leading down to the Vale of Ffestiniog. The slate-mining enclave of Blaenau Ffestiniog was excluded from the National Park because of the legacy of industrial dereliction which surrounds it.

Further south the rough heather-clad Rhinogs, which provide some of the toughest walking in Britain, and the Arennigs to the east, flank the beautiful valley of the Mawddach – one of the loveliest river valleys in Wales. Geologically speaking this area is known as the Harlech Dome, a great uplift of sedimentary rocks centred on the castle-crowned coastal town of

especially in the secret little Cwm Glas, with the jewel-like tarn of Glaslyn glittering at its heart.

The view from the summit, on a clear day, has not changed materially since Joseph Craddock described it in 1769: 'I doubt whether so extensive a circular prospect is to be seen in any part of the terraqueous globe', he wrote. One of the finest views I've ever had from the summit was shortly after midnight on a clear September evening, when the lights of Llanberis sparkled like a string of diamonds below our feet.

The classic excursion on Snowdon, reserved for experienced and well-equipped walkers only, is undoubtedly the famous Snowdon Horseshoe which takes in the knife-edge ridge of Crib-goch, Crib-y-ddysgl, Yr Wyddfa, Bwlch-y-Saethau and Y Lliwedd. South of the Snowdon massif, the bald moorland wastes of the Eifionydd and the Moelwyns are split by the Aberglaslyn Pass, with its famous and very attractive wooded

Harlech. The incredibly ancient Cambrian (the name comes from the old name for Wales) rocks of the Rhinogs are surrounded by the so-called 'ring of fire'. This is formed from the volcanic rocks of parts of Snowdon, the Glyders, the Carneddau, the Arrennigs and, to the south of Ffestiniog, the Arans and Cadair Idris. Cadair Idris (2,927ft/892m), overlooking the Mawddach estuary and the seaside town of Barmouth, may not top the magic 3000ft (914m) mark, but it is another favourite mountain and the ascent from Tal-y-Llyn to the wild mountain *cwm* of Cwm y Cau is one of the finest one-day walks in Snowdonia.

Of the lakes, or *llyns*, of Snowdonia perhaps Bala Lake (Llyn Tegid) at the foot of the Arans is the most famous and popular, but those surrounding Snowdon's summit are the most dramatically situated. Llyn Llydaw, crossed by the causeway used by the miners on their way to the copper mines under Yr Wyddfa's summit (hence the Miners' Track), winds seductively around the beetling crags of Lliwedd where snow patches linger long into the early summer, while Glaslyn, already described, is a little

The lace-like railway bridge across the Mawddach estuary, Barmouth

A distant view of the Snowdon Horseshoe from Llynnau Mymbyr lakes, Capel Curig

gem, and the traditional home of the Afangc, a mythical water monster.

The Afangc and those wild goats of Tryfan and the Rhinogs are not the only wildlife to be found in these forbidding mountain fastnesses. Snowdonia has no less than 17 National Nature Reserves (NNRs), more than any other National Park, and 45 Sites of Special Scientific Interest (SSSIs). Not far from the summit of Snowdon grows one of the rarest plants in Britain, *Lloydis serotina*, or the Snowdon lily, which was discovered here in 1696 by the pioneer Welsh botanist, Edward Lhuyd, and named after him.

Perhaps the most famous of Snowdonia's nature reserves is Cwm Idwal, the first to be declared in Wales. This classic glaciated cwm, split by the awesome gash of the Devil's Kitchen (Twll Du) at the foot of the Glyders and watched over by the noble peak of Y Garn, is the home of a wide range of arctic-alpine plants such as purple mountain saxifrage, moss campion, and that elusive Snowdon lily.

Llyn Idwal, dammed by a fine collection of rounded moraines left by

another mystery in these hills of myth and legend.

Just above Glaslyn at Bwlch y Saethau, on the col between Yr Wyddfa and Lliwedd, King Arthur is reputed to have fought his last battle with his treacherous nephew, Mordred. Mortally wounded on this 'Pass of the Arrows', Arthur was buried under a huge cairn known as Carnedd Arthur up until the last century.

With centres like Capel Curig on the eastern approach to Llanberis on the A5, Betws-y-Coed nestling in the forestry belt of the Gwydyr Forest on the eastern side of the Park, Dolgellau at the foot of Cadair Idris, and Harlech and Barmouth on the coast, the Snowdonia National Park is well served by good centres for the tourist. History buffs will delight in the string of fine castles, which include Harlech, Criccieth, Conwy and Caernarfon, built by Edward I in an attempt to subdue the restless Welsh. The strength of that fierce nationalism today shows how unsuccessful he and many subsequent invaders have been.

The Snowdon rack-and-pinion Mountain Railway taking on water at Clogwyn Station

an Ice Age glacier, is the winter home of whooper swans, pochard and goldeneye, while buzzards, ravens, merlins and the occasional peregrine soar overhead.

An ornithological oddity of Snowdonia is Craig yr Aderyn, or Bird Rock, overlooking the flat valley of the Dysynni near Tywyn. Here, on the precipitous, 200ft (61m) cliff face of the rock, 6 miles (9.6km) from the sea, nest sleek, black, reptilian-shaped cormorants. This is the only regular inland breeding site for cormorants in Britain and why it exists is yet

PEAK DISTRICT

The Peak District, sandwiched between the great industrial cities of
northern England, was the first British National Park to be
designated in 1951. It was an area where a National Park was most
needed, subjected, as it still is, to incredible pressures from mineral
extraction, development and public access. The Peak, standing at
the foot of the Pennines, is at the crossroads of Britain on the tran-
sition zone between the highlands and the lowlands. Because of
this it is a paradise for the naturalist, with wildlife from widely dif-
fering habitats coexisting side by side in a precious but pressurised
island of sharply contrasting landscapes.

Above, looking east down the valley of Edale from Rushup Edge, with Kinder Scout on the left

Right, A dry day at Kinder Downfall, the great waterfall on the western edge of Kinder Scout

Previous pages, Shutlingsloe, one of the few real peaks in the Peak District, from Shining Tor

I'll never forget my first visit to Kinder Scout, at 2,088ft (636m) the highest point of the 555 square mile (1,438 sq km) Peak National Park. The day wasn't promising. A thick grey blanket of cloud (known as 'clag' in these parts) lay heavily over the tops as we drove into the green valley of Edale to the start of the walk. However, as we had come a long way and were well equipped with map and compass we thought we'd give it a go.

The climb up from the typical little Pennine hamlet of Upper Booth, originally a Tudor cattle herdsman's shelter or vaccary, was pleasant enough and the weather even started to brighten – as it often can in these hills. There were occasional brief showers as we climbed steeply, accompanied by the constantly chattering Crowden Brook. Above us to the left, frowning down on the valley like the bastion of some medieval castle, stood Crowden Tower, one of Kinder's famous gritstone tors. The path disappeared in a jumble of rocks at the head of the clough as we struggled upwards, scrambling over enormous gritstone blocks and terraces to eventually emerge, sweating but triumphant, at the top. The scene which greeted our unbelieving eyes was staggering, and

it took what little of our breath was left clean away.

Before us as far as the eye could see stretched the most amazingly wild moonscape that either of us had ever seen. Wave after wave of banks of chocolate-brown peat, gently steaming in the now-strong sunlight, rolled away to the distant horizon, looking for all the world like a petrified ocean of manure.

John Hillaby, doyen of walking writers, described it perfectly in his *Journey Through Britain*. In a chapter entitled 'The Kinder Caper', he wrote: 'The top of Kinder Scout looks as if it's entirely covered in the droppings of dinosaurs'. The analogy, as far as we could see, was perfect.

When we'd got our breath back we walked west through the jumble of huge boulders behind Crowden Tower into another of Kinder's many surprises, known on the map as The Woolpacks. This amazing collection of weirdly shaped gritstone tors – some surrounded by a moat, others resembling anvils, chairs, toadstools, and even recumbent animals – is also known as Whipsnade and the Mushroom Garden, and it was easy to see why. In mist, these smooth, natural sculptures can take on a brooding, primeval quality which gives them a life of their own.

A Walk from Grindon to Butterton

This is a walk with superb views over the Manifold Valley and Dovedale to the hills of Derbyshire. About 6½ miles (10.5km) long, it is not too arduous although, like many valley areas, stream crossings on stepping stones can be affected dramatically by heavy rain.

DIRECTIONS

Park by Grindon village church and walk back towards the village, keeping left past the church gate – you can't cross the children's playground to do this. Descend the lane and turn left at the footpath sign. Continue down the field, over a brook, up into the next field, and over an unusual stile. Cross the road and another stile, then descend by a well-defined path into the valley bottom to a sign which indicates you are at the base of Ossoms Hill. Cross the footbridge, over a stile and immediately turn left and over another stile into Hoo Brook Valley, which you follow for ¼ mile (0.4km) on its right side before crossing a stile and stepping stones to continue with the valley on its left side. At some cottages, cross a stile, then the brook again, and follow the road to the end, crossing a ford onto the footpath on the other side. Turn right up this path and cross foot-bridges to save getting wet feet, as this is both a road and a stream

Derbyshire's lovely Manifold valley

bed. Climb up the quite steep hill and, shortly after passing the Manifold Arts and Craft Centre, bear right into a very narrow lane that will take you up to Butterton Church and the pub.

Black Lion Inn (Free House)
This welcoming, traditional village inn has a good reputation locally for both its food and beer. An ale house since 1782, it still retains a wealth of old beams and uneven floors that give it such character. There is a country dining room open on Friday and Saturday nights, and for Sunday lunch. Children are welcome.

On draught: Theakston Best and Old Peculier, Younger No 3, Scotch and Mild, Guinness, Becks, Taunton's Blackthorn and Autumn Gold ciders. Food: Blackboard menus in the bars offer frequently changing items such as broccoli and cheese pie, chicken curry and lasagne verde, liver and onion, and ploughmans with four different cheeses. Food is served from 12 to 2pm and from 7 to 9pm. Closed Wednesday lunchtime. Telephone: (05388) 232.

Leaving the pub, turn left then left again at the end of the car park, signposted to Onecote and Warslow. Just as the road starts to climb out of a dip, turn left onto a track and pass the front of Greenlow Head House, keeping left by the stone wall. Over a stile, walk through a narrow field and into another field which descends towards the valley bottom. Before you reach the corner of a wall, turn right towards a stile in a wall at the other side of the field. Keep on this clear footpath, through many stiles, to a brook just beyond a tiny cottage. Keep to the right of the barn and head straight up the hill, past another farm, to the main road. Turn left and in about ¼ mile (0.4km) turn right onto a track, immediately turning left and passing through a gate. Keep left, walk over a cattle-grid, and at the next gate turn left and continue alongside a fence, then a stone wall. Just after a long line of duckboards, climb over a stile then squeeze through the wall, turning left to follow this wall to another stile. Keep to the left of the farm, and stiles will take you over the farm track, directly towards Grindon Church, to the road. Cross, and follow the finger-post over the next wall. The path is fairly obvious and heads back directly to Grindon Church and your car.

Dovedale – one of the popular walking areas of the Peak National Park

appropriately known as bogtrotters – a new and entirely unexpected aspect.

There are really two distinct Peak Districts – two areas of equally beautiful but totally different landscapes, each of which has its own avid supporters. Kinder and the northern moors of Bleaklow and Black Hill, whose very names give away their hard, masculine nature, form the biggest block of what is known as the Dark Peak. The Dark Peak spreads around the northern, western and eastern sides of the National Park like an upturned horseshoe, while the softer, more feminine landscape of the White Peak occupies the centre and the south. It is a distinction based on the underlying geology of the area, for the

Chatsworth House, stately home of the Duke of Devonshire and known as the Palace of the Peak, with the Emperor Fountain

As we climbed down the ancient packhorse route of Jacob's Ladder, named not after the biblical figure but much more prosaically after Jacob Marshall, a local farmer who first cut the steps into the hillside in the 17th century, we reflected that Kinder was certainly different and unlike anywhere else we'd been in Britain. I have climbed up Kinder's craggy sides many times since then, and every time I see or experience something entirely different. That is the attraction of Kinder Scout and the high northern moors of the Peak District – they always have this magnificent sense of age-old permanence, yet on every visit they show their devotees –

Dark Peak moors, tors and edges (escarpments) are formed by sombre-coloured millstone grit and the White Peak plateau and dales from pearly-white limestone. Both rocks are sedimentary, laid down during the carboniferous period about 350 million years ago when the land we now know as Britain was much closer to the equator.

The limestone is the fossilised remains of countless millions of tiny sea creatures and organisms which were laid down in a shallow, semi-tropical sea. This was later overlaid with mud and grit deposited by a huge prehistoric river, forming the grits, shales and sandstones of the Dark Peak. Countless millions of years of erosion by wind, water and ice have gradually and remorselessly removed the gritstone cover from the centre and south of the Peak, revealing the dazzling white limestone skeleton beneath. This is all the stuff of textbook geology, making the Peak a popular place for students of that science.

However, you don't have to be a geologist to appreciate the landscapes of Britain's first National Park. The 22 million day visits it receives every year show it to be one of the most popular National Parks not only in Britain, but the world, and the area it covers seems to have something for just about everybody. Visitors come to the Peak for many reasons, but for

The courtyard of Haddon Hall, one of the most perfectly preserved medieval manor houses in England

Above, looking south down Dovedale from Thorpe Cloud

Right, Monsal Dale viaduct from Monsal Head, with Fin Cop to the left

most it provides the chance to escape into beautiful, unspoilt countryside from the towns and cities of the north and Midlands. It is sometimes hard to believe as you look out across the wild moorland heights of Kinder or Bleaklow that just over a dozen miles (19km) in either direction, east or west, are the city centres of Manchester and Sheffield. This accessibility is at once one of the Peak's great attractions, and one of its greatest problems. The sheer number of those visitors can cause congestion in the small villages and narrow country roads, and erosion on a massive scale on some of the most popular footpaths, notably the Pennine Way which starts its 250 mile (400km) journey north at Edale.

The moors and dales of the Peak were not always as easily accessible as they are today. In the 1930s the highest and wildest moors of the Dark Peak, including Kinder and Bleaklow, were out of bounds to the rambler because they were strictly preserved grouse moors, watched over by patrolling gamekeepers. The 1932 Mass Trespass on Kinder Scout, after which five ramblers were imprisoned, saw the

start of the end of that restriction and today, thanks to access agreements negotiated by the National Park with landowners, over 80 square miles (207 sq km) have open access.

Yet bogtrotting across the moors is not everyone's cup of tea and many people prefer the gentler walking available on the 4,000 miles (6,400km) of public rights of way in the National Park. Many of these are on the limestone plateau of the White Peak, where pretty stone-built villages like Bakewell, Tideswell, Hartington, Foolow and Monyash seem to grow almost organically from the landscape. Others pass through the spectacular, crag-rimmed limestone dales of the White Peak, home of the rarest and best of the Peak's wildlife, which have been famous as visitor attractions since the 17th century.

The best known of these dales is undoubtedly Dovedale, the praises of which were first extolled by Izaak Walton and Charles Cotton in the anglers' bible, *The Compleat Angler*, first published in 1653. Walton dubbed the Dove 'the princess of rivers', and tourists have been agreeing with him ever since. But many other dales, such

as Lathkill Dale (part of the Derbyshire Dales National Nature Reserve), Bradford Dale, near Youlgreave, and the Manifold valley, just over the border in Staffordshire, are equally beautiful and often not as crowded as Dovedale, especially in high summer.

The first real tourist guide to the Peak was written by Thomas Hobbes, philosopher and tutor to the Cavendish family at Chatsworth, whose *De Mirabilibus Pecci*, or *The Wonders of the Peak*, published in 1636, became the basis for a generally accepted Grand Tour of the region. Charles Cotton of Hartington, co-author of *The Compleat Angler*, later rehashed Hobbes's seven 'wonders' in

Autumn on Curbar Edge, looking down the Derwent valley towards Baslow Edge

his own version, published in 1681. Nearly all these wonders were in the White Peak, and they included places like Peak Cavern, the largest cave entrance in Britain at Castleton, Poole's Cavern in Buxton, and Eldon Hole, a large open pothole near Peak Forest. Mam Tor was included because of its unstable east face which constantly sheds rocks and debris, earning it the nickname the 'Shivering Mountain', and another wonder was the palatial home of the Dukes of Devonshire at Chatsworth, newly won from the wilderness.

For many people coming from the south, the east or the Midlands, the introduction to the Peak and the Pennines is the White Peak, and the first thing that strikes these visitors from the lowland shires is the intricate system of drystone walls which spreads across the green pastures like a net. It has been estimated that, in the White Peak alone, there are 26,000 miles (41,600km) of drystone walls which, if built around the equator, would more than encircle the earth. These are mostly a legacy from the Enclosure Movements of the 18th and 19th centuries, although some have recently

been archaeologically dated to the Roman period. Certainly, early man found the Peak very much to his liking and the area is a rich treasure-house for the archaeologist and landscape historian. Almost every hilltop in this part of the Peak paradoxically carries the name low, which denotes a tumulus or burial mound, usually dating from the Bronze Age. Even earlier is the famous Neolithic stone circle, or henge, of Arbor Low, near Monyash, which has been dubbed the Stonehenge of the North. But Arbor Low's stones, unlike those of its Wiltshire contemporary, lie recumbent within a grassy embankment which has a Bronze Age barrow on its rim.

Later in the Bronze Age there seems to have been a movement towards the apparently inhospitable moors of the Dark Peak and in places like the Eastern Moor, west of Chesterfield and Sheffield, entire self-contained communities of this period have been identified. The reason for this movement is thought to have been related to a change in the climate of Britain, and weather conditions were certainly more amenable. Today, the area is only home to hawk and hare.

Bakewell's 14th-century bridge over the River Wye leads the eye to the spire of All Saints parish church

The Ladybower Reservoir impounds the waters of the Upper River Derwent in the north-east of the Park

One of the largest and highest Iron Age hillforts in the Pennines is found at Mam Tor, at the head of the broad Hope valley on the boundary between the White and Dark Peak. On this windswept, 1,695ft (517m) hill of shale and grit a sizeable population once lived, perhaps using their 'town in the sky' as a summertime shelter from which they could watch over their flocks of grazing animals. It is one of several hillforts which are scattered about the Dark Peak, usually overlooking the broad river valleys which separate it from the lush pastures of the limestone country.

The Romans came to the Peak to exploit the easily accessible veins of lead ore which criss-cross the White Peak. Their lead-mining centre, which we know from surviving pigs (ingots) of lead was called *Ludutarum*, has still not been satisfactorily identified, and the only sizeable Roman settlement which has been excavated is the small fortlet of Navio at Brough, a few miles from Mam Tor in the Hope valley, which may have been built to defend those lead-mining interests. But the

heyday of the lead-mining industry in the Peak was during the 18th century when over 10,000 miners were at work in the White Peak area. The great landowners of the Peak, such as the Dukes of Devonshire at Chatsworth and the Dukes of Rutland from nearby Haddon Hall, gained much of their wealth from the mineral rights exploited by mining in the Peak and they left a legacy of rolling parkland and beautiful stately homes which adorn the valleys of the Derwent and the Wye.

The Peak has always been a dynamic, working landscape, and wherever the visitor looks he will see evidence of man's hand. The huge limestone quarries, such as those which excluded Buxton and Matlock from the boundaries of the National Park, are still very visible features from the Park, and an important source of employment for the 38,000 residents.

Even in the apparently wildest places, such as the valley of the Upper Derwent in the shadow of Bleaklow, the landscape of lake and forest is the

result of human activities. The triple reservoirs of Howden, Derwent and Ladybower were created to provide water for the growing industrial populations of the surrounding cities, and the trees were planted to protect water purity. Today, they are popular places for visitors and the subject of a traffic management scheme similar to one first introduced in the Goyt valley on the western side of the Park. Other pioneering projects by the independent National Park authority have included the transformation of derelict railway lines, such as the Tissington and High Peak Trails, into pleasant walking and riding routes. So, despite the pressures, the Peak still provides the Great Escape to the citizens of the surrounding cities.

Thorpe Cloud, a limestone reef knoll at the southern end of Dovedale, commands fine views

YORKSHIRE DALES

'There Must be Dales in Paradise.' The incorrigible fell-wanderer
Alfred J Brown was in no doubt when he penned a poem with this
title in 1928; and for the citizens of the wool towns and cities of the
former West Riding, the Yorkshire Dales have always been the
closest thing to an earthly paradise. The subtle, enchanting mixture
of broad dales with moorland above and mellow villages and
barns springing harmoniously from the valley floor, some of the
most spectacular limestone scenery in Britain, and secret, sylvan
waterfalls hidden away in the recesses of the hills, all combine to
make the Yorkshire Dales a very special place.

Late afternoon sun lights Pen-y-Ghent, one of the Three Peaks above Horton in Ribblesdale

Previous pages, fretted limestone pavements above Malham Cove, in the Yorkshire Dales

The walk up through the grounds of the Ingleborough Estate at Clapham had been a joy, the well-engineered path decorated by banks of wood anemones, primroses and dog's mercury on the floor of the mixed woodland on either side. Here and there, contrasting sharply with the native oak and ash, were the more exotic rhododendrons and azaleas introduced by the pioneer traveller and botanist, Reginald Farrer, whose home was at Ingleborough Hall. Passing by the ornamental lake (whose harnessed waters gave Clapham the first electric street lights in the north-west of England in 1896) we climbed steadily through Clapdale Wood and out on to the open pastures of Clapham Beck towards Beck Head and the dark entrance of Ingleborough Cave. The present entrance was made in 1837 by Farrer's father, a keen amateur potholer, and it was one of the first show caves to be opened in the Dales. Ingleborough has some spectacular and beautiful formations, but our destination that day lay high on the moorland above, where the waters from Fell Beck,

gushing out from the hillside just beyond the entrance to the show cave, first disappear into the Dales' 'underground'.

Crossing the bridge, we walked on into a narrowing dale where the walls of limestone gradually began to crowd in, blocking out the sun. After crossing a ladder-stile we turned sharply left into the confines of Trow Gill, one of the scenic wonders of the Dales. Now steep, glistening limestone cliffs, topped by a crest of straggling pines, overhung the path as it narrowed to become a scramble up a boulder choke.

At last we emerged on to the moorland of Clapham Bottoms and followed the line of the infant Clapham Beck over another stile, with the brooding shape of Ingleborough, topped by a threatening cloud.

Ingleborough is perhaps the most famous hill in Yorkshire – it is said that every Yorkshireman must climb to its broad flat, 2,373ft (723m) summit before he dies – and it is one of the now infamous Three Peaks. (Its hillfort-capped summit is where the Iron Age tribe of the Brigantes, led by Venutius, are supposed to have held

Cottages at Grassington, the 'capital' of Upper Wharfedale

Standing four-square against the elements, Bolton Castle lords it over Wensleydale

out against the invading Romans.) With the nearby hills of Whernside (2415ft/736m) and Pen-y-Ghent (2277ft/694m), Ingleborough is a milestone on the classic one-day walking excursion in the Dales – the 26 mile (42km) Three Peaks Walk. However, such has been the popularity of this tough challenge that the National Park authority has had to cope with terrible problems of erosion on the footpaths between the three. Over £1 million has already been spent on a massive programme of footpath restoration, and most responsible ramblers now give the route a wide berth in order to give the battered landscape a well-earned rest.

As we approached a shallow, saucer-like depression in the moor, we saw through the spitting rain that it was filled with the brightly coloured anoraks of about 100 people. The object of their attention on this 'claggy' day on the slopes of Ingleborough lay at their feet – the awesome, yawning chasm of Gaping Gill, the biggest pothole in Britain. Here, Fell Beck plunges 360ft (109m) into an underground cavern big enough, it is said, to hold York Minster.

This was a bank holiday (as the weather might have indicated), which is one of the few times every year that mere non-caving mortals can be winched down by local caving clubs into the depths of Gaping Gill. We dutifully queued in the now constant drizzle, awaiting our turn to be strapped in the bosun's chair which would take us, quite literally, into the heart of the Dales. Eventually our turn came, and as we lurched off into space we were carried through the cascading waters of Fell Beck and out of the grey daylight into the ever-deepening darkness. The joke among the cavers is that there is no charge for taking you to the bottom of Gaping Gill; but there is a fee for bringing you back! Once at the boulder-strewn bottom, our eyes soon became accustomed to the darkness and we were able to appreciate the vastness of the enormous, spray-lit cavern in which we stood. It remains one of the great experiences of the Yorkshire Dales.

In limestone country such as this there are really two landscapes. Above ground there are the great scenic show-places such as the sweeping, 300ft (91m) amphitheatre of Malham Cove and its neighbouring, even more impressive, Gothic gorge of Gordale Scar. Then there are the great cliffs, scars and pavements of places such as Kilnsey Crag in Upper Wharfedale, where the leaning, overhanging crag marks the passage of the cutting edge of an Ice Age glacier but which never fails to remind me of the white hood of one of the Cistercian monks from Fountains Abbey. In medieval times the monks governed all this land as an enormous sheep ranch and gained the wealth required to build their abbeys, which are beautiful even in decay.

Below ground is the other splendour of the Dales, created by the porous nature of limestone and the chemical effect which rainwater has on it. Most visitors are content to be guided round the well-lit show caves of Ingleborough, or White Scar on the other side of Ingleborough near Ingleton, but to the pot-holer, the Yorkshire Dales are another kind of

Settle, seen here from Castleberg Hill, is just outside the National Park at the foot of Ribblesdale

The great overhanging limestone crag of Kilnsey, in Upper Wharfedale

paradise with miles of underground passageways still waiting to be explored.

Like other Pennine landscapes, the bones of the Yorkshire Dales were mainly formed during the carboniferous period, perhaps 350 million years ago. The limestone, laid down in a tropical sea, was later overlaid by the shales and grits from a vast northern river, and this sequence resulted in the distinctive, stepped shape of many of the major dales and the noble, crouching-lion profiles of hills like Ingleborough and Pen-y-Ghent. Ice, rain and rivers have worn away most of the shale and grit cover in the Dales, leaving the harder, more resistant 'steps' on the slopes above. Geologists know this regular, almost rhythmic, succession as the Yoredale Series, which takes its name from

Wensleydale's old name. The exceptions to this regularity are the smooth slopes of the Howgill Fells, tucked away near Sedbergh in the north-west corner of the Yorkshire Dales National Park. The Park was set up in 1954 and, at 683 square miles (1,769 sq km), is the third largest. In geological terms, the Howgills are much more closely related to the smooth slates of the northern Lake District, formed of Silurian rock laid down in a much earlier epoch.

This geological backbone gives the Yorkshire Dales its gritty character, and it also provides many of its 18,600 residents with a livelihood. At the same time, it poses the National Park authority with one of its greatest problems. Wherever an easily obtainable rock such as limestone breaks the surface you will find

quarries, and the Yorkshire Dales has ten of these, seen to worst effect around Horton-in-Ribblesdale and in Wharfedale. While recognising that the industry is an important, although decreasing, local source of employment, the National Park authority is concerned that this chemically-pure rock often ends up merely as aggregate – for which almost any rock could be – used under the tarmac of a new road.

Mining and quarrying have been staple industries in the Dales for centuries, although never on the enormous scale of modern quarrying. Swaledale, the northernmost and perhaps the most remote and beautiful of the dales, was once the centre of a thriving lead-mining industry, the remains of which can still be inspected in places like Gunnerside Gill and Swinner Gill. Evidence of 't'owd man', as the old lead mines are known, can still be seen in many other dales.

In fact the oldest, most obvious and least harmful industry in the Dales is farming, and it is this which has largely shaped the landscape of the Yorkshire Dales we know today. The intricate pattern of drystone-walled fields and neat gritstone barns, usually about one for every two fields, is the most characteristic landscape of the Dales, and is perhaps best seen in Swaledale or the upper parts of Ribblesdale.

The wonderful hay meadows of dales like Wensleydale, Wharfedale or Swaledale, starred with wildflowers

The distinctive Dales pattern of walls and barns at Gunnerside, in Swaledale

and humming with insects in early summer, are one of the delights of the Yorkshire Dales. The National Park authority does what it can to encourage this traditional form of farming, which has been carried on for hundreds of years, and if barns become redundant they are converted to bunkhouses for visitors.

One of the most fascinating features of the Yorkshire Dales is the astonishing continuity which can be read in the landscape. Placenames are an important clue, and nowhere else in Britain can such an absorbing story of continuous residence be traced through names on the map. The earliest Norse invaders came to the Dales from the west, from the Lake District and from Ireland, and generally settled in the higher and wilder parts of the Dales which were the closest thing, in landscape terms, to their Scandinavian homelands. So the modern visitor will find pure Norse words like *gill*, or *beck* (stream), *fell* (hillside), *foss* (waterfall) and

thwaite (clearing), in placenames scattered across the landscape.

Further down the Dales, however, the gentler, more wooded landscapes of the broad, fertile river valleys were more suited to the Anglian and Danish settlers who left a legacy of village names ending in *-by*, *-thorp* or *-ley*. It has been said that an experienced observer can tell not only which dale a man comes from, but which part of that dale, just by listening to his accent. River names such as the Swale, Ure, Ribble and Wharfe, and those of the major hills such as Pen-y-Ghent, and Pen Hill in Wensleydale, are much older, named in Celtic times by the first inhabitants who wanted to identify such features.

Many of the nine million annual visitors to the Yorkshire Dales National Park go to honeypot villages such as Malham, Grassington, Hawes or Sedbergh – all splendid examples of Pennine settlements and generally unspoilt by insensitive development. Visitors also throng to the popular

Linton Falls on the River Wharfe, near Grassington

tourist sights of Malham Cove (which once boasted a waterfall higher than Niagara); the pretty Aysgarth Falls in Upper Wensleydale; the landscaped grounds of Bolton Abbey, with its famous stepping stones and Strid rapids in Wharfedale; or the impressive 100ft (30m) single-drop waterfall of Hardraw Force, approached through the Green Dragon Inn at Hardraw.

The motorist can reach many of these beauty spots, as well as some of the wilder parts of the Dales like the Buttertubs Pass at the head of Swaledale, because the broader Yorkshire Dales (unlike those of the Peak) are usually threaded by

Southerscales Scar, an extensive area of limestone pavements, with mighty Ingleborough in the background

The packhorse bridge over Clapham Beck in the village of Clapham, at the foot of Ingleborough

good roads. The Dales also boasts one of the most spectacular railway lines in Britain – the Settle and Carlisle, which passes through some of the finest scenery in the Dales on its 72 mile (115km) journey. The story of the fight by railway buffs and local people to keep this ambitious line open was one of the great conservationist victories of the 1980s, and, with the line as popular as it has ever been, its immediate future seems secure. This journey through the Dales is not to be missed, and it provides a superb link for walkers using linear rather than circular routes, wanting to return to their car.

With its 325 bridges, 21 viaducts, 14 tunnels and 20 stations, the 'S and C', as it is affectionately known, was the last of the great navvy-built railways, and a considerable triumph for Victorian civil engineering. The most famous of the viaducts, and the symbol of the fight to save the line, is the 24-arched Ribblehead Viaduct, a landmark in the heart of Three Peaks country. Many of the stations are some miles from the villages they serve because of the difficult nature of the route, which opened to passengers in 1876. The National Park authority recently made the whole of the S & C a conservation area – undoubtedly the longest in the country – in order to protect its continuity. Through its integrated Dalesrail service which is linked to local buses, much of the Dales has been opened up to public transport and as a result eased traffic congestion on the roads.

However, the Yorkshire Dales National Park is walkers' country *par excellence*, and walking remains the finest way to see it. No one knew this better than the famous writer J B Priestley, a native of Bradford, who described the Dales in his *English Journey* (1934) with the words:

'I know no other countryside that offers you such entrancing variety. So if you can use your legs and have a day now and then to yourself, you never need to be unhappy long in Bradford.'

The Dales, he said, had bred a race of mighty pedestrians, and none was mightier than Alfred J Brown, whose earlier book, *Moorland Tramping* (1931), remains a classic among walking guides. It was Brown who patriotically enthused in his *Four Boon Fellows*, published in 1928:

There *must* be dales in Paradise
Which you and I will find,
And walk together dalesman-wise
And smile (since God is kind)
At all the foreign peoples there
Enchanted by our blessed air!

Garsdale Viaduct, on the Settle–Carlisle railway, looking towards Mallerstang Edge

LAKE DISTRICT

The Lake District could be said to be where the National Park movement began. In one of the first guidebooks to the area, William Wordsworth wrote that 'persons of pure taste' would 'deem the district a sort of national property, in which every man has a right and interest who has an eye to perceive and a heart to enjoy'. It was to be another 150 years before Wordsworth's dream became a reality, and the Lake District became Britain's largest National Park. Today it is the same enchantingly beautiful, accessible landscape of craggy mountains, shining lakes and reed-fringed tarns which first entranced Wordsworth and his fellow poets of the Romantic school.

only for being the wildest, most barren and frightful of any that I have passed over in England, or even in Wales itself...' He saw nothing but 'an inhospitable terror' in the Lakeland hills and, reflecting the feelings of his day, he added that it was 'of no advantage to represent horror as the character of a country...'

Defoe was not alone in expressing his feelings in this way. Dr John Brown, describing the vale and lake of Keswick in 1769, saw only 'rocks and

William Wordsworth's former home at Dove Cottage, Grasmere, is now a museum

*I*t was in his best-selling *Guide Through the District of the Lakes in the North of England*, first published in 1810, that William Wordsworth made the suggestion that it should become 'a sort of national property', a statement which is now generally regarded as the genesis of the National Park movement. It was Wordsworth, too, who started the more general appreciation of the Lake District as a place to visit with his guide which, 180 years later, is still in print. He broke the mould of previous guidebooks which, with one or two notable exceptions, had regarded this craggy, mountainous area with something approaching mortal terror. It should be remembered that before Wordsworth and his fellow Romantics began to find beauty and inspiration in rugged, natural scenery like that of the Lakes, such places were universally regarded as blots, rather than beauty spots, on the landscape.

The earliest travellers to the Lakes were filled with fear and trepidation as they cautiously made their way, using guides, into these 'horrid' and 'frightful' places. One of the first was the journalist Daniel Defoe, who wrote in his *Tour Through the Whole Island of Great Britain* (1724) that Westmorland was 'a country eminent

Previous pages, evening calm on England's largest lake, Windermere

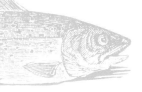

cliffs of stupendous heights, hanging broken over the lake in horrible grandeur'. Thomas Gray, author of the famous *Elegy Written in a Country Churchyard*, also dared go no further into the jaws of Borrowdale, explaining to his readers that 'all farther access is here barr'd to prying Mortals'. William Gilpin described the ascent of Dunmail Raise from Grasmere thus: 'The whole view is entirely of the horrid kind... Of all the scenes I ever saw, this was the most adapted to the perpetration of some dreadful deed.' Yet more and more 'persons of pure taste' were finding pleasure in picturesque landscapes, encouraged by artists like J M W Turner, John Constable and Thomas Gainsborough who, quite literally, were putting the Lakes in the picture. As the appreciation of landscape increased, a movement – led by Wordsworth and the school of writers attracted to the Lakes by his poetry – to preserve it all began.

Wild daffodils in Gowbarrow Park, on the shores of Ullswater

Wordsworth was also the first of the upper-class preservationists who really wanted to keep the scenery just for themselves. They feared the results of allowing, as he put it, 'artisans, labourers and the humbler class of shopkeeper' into the area. When an extension of the main railway line to Kendal and Windermere was proposed, he fumed in a famous sonnet:

> Is then no nook of English ground
>   secure
> From rash assault?

This elitist attitude was to become a common one among Wordsworth's fellow Romantics. Later John Ruskin, who lived for the last years of his life at Brantwood beside Coniston Water, complained of 'the certainty of the deterioration of the moral character in the inhabitants of every district penetrated by a railway'. He objected to the railway engineers 'making a steam merry-go-round of the lake country', and as for the resultant incoming tourists, Ruskin declared imperiously: 'I don't want them to see Helvellyn while they are drunk'. Despite these apparent double standards, it was from among this social class that the first moves to protect the Lake District came. Canon

Hardwicke Rawnsley, incumbent at Crosthwaite near Keswick, became one of the founding fathers of the National Trust. Now the biggest single private landowner in the 885 square mile (2,292 sq km) National Park, the Trust owns about a third of the area and manages it in a way which would no doubt delight those early pioneer preservationists.

People such as Rawnsley were also great walkers, and this tradition has been perpetuated to this day by the works of the late Alfred Wainwright (among others), former borough treasurer at Kendal, whose immaculately hand-crafted but sadly unrevised *Pictorial Guides to the Lakeland Fells* now rival Wordsworth's guide in sales. Thomas de Quincey, the opium-smoking poet who was a close friend of the Wordsworths and took over the lease of Dove Cottage at Grasmere when William and his devoted sister, Dorothy, moved out to Rydal Mount, estimated that William's legs, which he describes as 'certainly not ornamental', covered between 175,000 (280,000km) and 180,000 miles (288,000km) in his lifetime.

Samuel Taylor Coleridge, another of the Lakes School, is credited with undertaking one of the first recorded rock climbs in the area when he successfully negotiated a descent via

Below, Tarn Hows, near Hawkshead, a man-made but charming landscape of lakes and trees

Right, a pleasure steamer at Bowness-on-Windermere

A Literary Landscape

Main picture: William
Wordsworth, doyen of the
Lake Poets
Below: close friend and
collaborator on 'Lyrical
Ballads', Samuel Taylor
Coleridge

The poet Wordsworth was a
prime mover in both the
early popularisation and the
preservation of the Lake District, and
for many visitors the region is
inseparable from the images created
by Wordsworth and his fellow Lake
Poets of the Romantic Age, Coleridge
and Southey. Others come here to
see the countryside portrayed in
such minute and beautiful detail by
the children's author Beatrix Potter,
who lived for many years at Hill Top,
Near Sawrey, or to discover the land
of adventure which featured so
strongly in the stories of Arthur
Ransome. More recently, the Lake
District has appeared as the setting
for popular novels by Richard Adams
and Melvyn Bragg.

Yet William Wordsworth, who was
born and brought up in the market

town of Cockermouth, in the north-western corner of the National Park, is still the linchpin of literary Lakeland. His early experiences of nature and the land around him – so vividly recalled in *The Prelude*, perhaps his greatest work – influenced his writing throughout his long life (born in 1770, he died in 1850). Working with Samuel Taylor Coleridge, he developed a new style of poetry, considered accessible to all, with which to communicate his ideas about man and nature and their influences upon each other. Wordsworth attended school at Hawkshead (where he carved his initials into one of the old wooden desks), and in 1799 settled with his devoted sister Dorothy at Dove Cottage in Grasmere, where they were to live for nine years. During this time Dorothy started her famous Grasmere journal, and her close and lively observations of nature proved a strong influence on both her

brother and Coleridge, a frequent visitor. After William's marriage, the family eventually moved to Rydal Mount, and both homes are open to visitors. The family is buried together in the churchyard at Grasmere.

The Wordsworths and their writing attracted many other famous authors to the Lake District, which became a hive of literary activity, perceived all at once as a desirable place to live in and visit – authors such as Sir Walter Scott, Charlotte Brontë and John Keats included the Lakes in their tours of the country, and John Ruskin, the celebrated Victorian critic of art, architecture and society made his home at Brantwood, on the shores of Coniston Water. Brantwood, which contains a large collection of his drawings and paintings, is open to visitors, and the Ruskin Museum in Coniston village is dedicated to the great man and his circle.

Boat moorings at Lakeside, Keswick, looking across Derwentwater towards Causey Pike, right, and Catbells

Broad Stand after climbing Scafell Pike, at 3,206 feet (977m) the highest point in England, while on a 100 mile (160km) walking tour in 1802.

It was to be another 84 years before the sport of rock climbing was launched in the Lake District by Walter Haskett Smith's solo ascent of Napes Needle, the sharply pointed pinnacle on the side of 2,949ft (899m) high Great Gable. In his graphic account of that pioneering climb, Smith described himself as 'feeling as small as a mouse climbing a milestone'.

Rock climbing, especially in Borrowdale and Wasdale, still attracts large numbers of climbers to the Lakes, but the majority of the estimated 20 million annual visitors to this most famous British National Park, set up in 1951, follow in Wordsworth's and Wainwright's steps and wander the fells on foot. With free and open access to most of the hills, and a well- maintained and signposted

network of 1,500 miles (2,400km) of public rights of way in the valleys, there is a lifetime of walking within the boundaries of the Park. However, pressure on the most popular paths inevitably brings problems in its wake, and major restoration work has had to be undertaken by both the National Park authority and the National Trust to combat the effects of human erosion. Staircases of natural rock have had to be installed on popular summits such as Helm Crag, near the Wordsworths' home at Grasmere, perhaps realising some of the fears of Wordsworth and Ruskin.

Other honeypots to be avoided on busy summer weekends are Windermere, where a 10mph (16kph) speed limit was recently imposed on England's biggest lake to curb water-skiers and powerboats; Tarn Hows, the quaint village set in a pretty, though man-made, landscape near the village of Hawkshead where William Wordsworth went to school; and the Langdale valley, where the twin-topped Langdale Pikes provide an irresistible lure for the hill walker.

Wordsworth, a keen observer of the landscape, was the first to compare the topography of the Lake District to the radiating spokes of a wheel, and the mountains and dales, most containing lakes or tarns, do seem to spread out from a central point around about Dunmail Raise, the highest point on the A591 between Grasmere and Keswick. The Lake District's most distinguished modern poet, Norman Nicholson, has more accurately compared the shape with that of a lemon-squeezer because the dales are gouged out of a dome and slope outwards to a lower rim.

Three major types of rock are encountered in the Lake District. The

Coniston village, looking towards the Coniston Fells

Loweswater is a little-visited lake on the far west of the National Park

Silurian slates create the softer, well-wooded landscapes found around Windermere and Coniston Water in the south, while the Borrowdale volcanics, dating from the Ordovician period, give the rugged, craggy features of Borrowdale, Langdale, Helvellyn and Wasdale in the central part of the district. The older Skiddaw slates have created the steep but usually smooth shapes of the northern fells which include Skiddaw, Blencathra and Grisedale Pike, and which echo the Howgill Fells across the Lune Gorge. Surrounding the Park is a border of carboniferous limestone.

The most important agent which shaped the Lake District we see today was the enormous crushing, grinding, chiselling power of Ice Age glaciers. Centred on the middle of the district

for several thousand years, they created the 'radiating wheel' formation first noted by Wordsworth, and scooped out the U-shaped dales within which most of the lakes now lie. Everywhere you look you can see signs of the passing glaciers which did not disappear until about 10,000 years ago – relatively recently in the vast geological timescale. The strange, rounded, grassy hillocks – drumlins – which can be seen alongside the A591 at Dunmail Raise were left by the retreating glaciers, and from the summit of the pass, between the summits of Seat Sandal and Steel Fell, the classic U-shape of glaciated valleys is very evident.

Up in the hills, usually on the north or north-eastern slopes of the mountains, corries (locally known as

Rydal Water, glimpsed through the silver birches of White Moss Common

coves) have been scooped out by snow and glacial action, often leaving a jewel-like tarn at their heart. Good examples can be seen at Red Tarn on Helvellyn, Scales Tarn on Blencathra, Levers Water on Coniston Old Man, and Blea Water, the deepest of all, on the High Street range above the flooded vale of Haweswater.

The pedant will tell you that, in fact, there is only one lake in the Lake District because Bassenthwaite Lake in the north-west of the National Park is the only one actually called a lake. All the rest take the older names of mere, or water, and the smaller lakes, the tarns, take their name from the Old Norse word, *tjorn*. Many other Norse names crop up on the Lake District map, such as *thwaite*, meaning a clearing for pasture; *fell*, meaning a

mountain; and *seat*, meaning a hill pasture used in the summer. The abundance of these ancient names shows the origins of the early farmers and shepherds of these hills, although they were not the first to walk the fells by any means.

One of the most atmospheric places in the Lake District is the Neolithic stone circle at Castlerigg, a few miles outside Keswick. Here, on an elevated pasture backed by the smooth slopes of Blencathra and Skiddaw to the north and the Helvellyn range to the south, stands the most impressive prehistoric monument in the National Park. Described by John Keats on a visit in 1818 as 'A dismal cirque of Druid stones upon a forlorn moor', Castlerigg is thought to have been some kind of religious centre, but no-one can be sure. Evidence of prehistoric industrial activity was found in 1947 on the steep scree slopes below Pike of Stickle, one of the Langdale Pikes. Here the site of a stone

Looking down from the heights of Hardknott Pass into Eskdale

axe factory was identified. These elegant tools were literally at the cutting edge of Stone Age technology and the craftsmen who shaped them certainly knew their geology for they chose the fine-grained, hardened tuff found among the Borrowdale volcanics for their raw material. The axes, which were later exported all over Britain, were finally shaped and finished at sites on the coast. Since the Langdale discovery several other axe factories have been identified, one close to the summit of Scafell Pike – surely the highest industrial site in Britain.

The Romans also stamped their imperial mark on the Lake District and when motorists embark on one of the most exciting car drives in Britain, across the Wrynose and Hardknott Passes between Ambleside and Ravenglass, they are following in the footsteps of the Roman legions who built forts at either end of the route. Just below the head of the pass, on a green 800ft (243m) spur under Border End, are the well-preserved remains of the Roman fort of *Mediobogdum*, one of the most remote and impressive Roman sites in Britain.

However, it was Viking raiders from the north who first tamed the wild Lake District landscape, and nowhere gives a better impression of a Norse settlement than the tiny hamlet of Watendlath, high above the deep, wooded vale of Borrowdale, just south of Derwent Water. The name is thought to mean 'the barn at the end of the lake', and it is still a pretty accurate description of the spot today. A collection of grey-stoned farm buildings cluster round the head of a reed-fringed tarn at the end of a narrow, dead-end road which winds up past the popular viewpoint of Ashness Bridge, above Derwent Water. Hills with Norse names such as High Seat, Great Crag and Rough Knott frown down on the secret valley which looks as if it has been transported from Arctic Norway. When I last visited Watendlath with the family we walked across the fells to the beautiful little rowan-fringed Dock Tarn and found it decorated by the white flowers of waterlilies. I wasn't at all surprised to discover later that the name came from the Old Norse and meant 'the tarn of the waterlilies'.

Grasmoor, seen from the rocky shores of Crummock Water

NORTH YORK MOORS

The crowning glory of the North York Moors is its heather moorland, which covers about 40 per cent of the National Park and forms the largest expanse of heather in England. It is seen to best effect in late summer when the rolling horizons of the high central moors are covered in a dusty pink cloak. Tucked away on the shoulder of north-east England and rising suddenly from the Vale of York, the North York Moors has always seemed to be a place apart. Yet the moorland is only part of the story; secluded wooded dales and a spectacular 25 mile (40km) stretch of coastline, which includes the highest cliffs on the east coast, complete the entrancing picture.

Previous pages, the view into Farndale from Blakey Ridge, North York Moors

Writing in the 12th century, St Ailred, third abbot of Rievaulx Abbey in Ryedale on the edge of the North York Moors, said he had found there 'peace, everywhere serenity and a marvellous freedom from the tumult of the world'. What better recommendation could there be for a National Park?

The North York Moors became the sixth National Park to be designated, in 1952, and covers 554 square miles (1,435 sq km) of the Cleveland, Hambleton and Tabular Hills of North Yorkshire, plus 25 miles (40km) of North Sea coastline which includes part of the Cleveland Way long-distance path. Due to its position on the east coast of England, the North York Moors receives much less rainfall than the other upland National Parks,

Rocky outcrops on Castleton Rigg (ridge), above Castleton in Esk Dale

but the same geographical location makes it a cold place in winter, and blizzards often block the roads that cross the bleak, central moorland heights.

The North York Moors is probably one of the most under-rated of our National Parks, but with 11 million visits annually more and more people are discovering how much the area has to offer. Perhaps more than any other, the North York Moors National Park authority has embraced the fact that a properly managed and sustainable 'green' tourism industry can bring sound economic benefits to the 25,000-strong resident population.

With the enormous industrial area of Teesside just to the north, the Park also has an important role to play in the regeneration of an area of Britain

which has suffered more than most from the effects of the recession. It also remains a vital 'lung' to the sprawling populations of Middlesbrough, Billingham, and the other Tees-side towns.

It is a strange fact that two of the most obvious features of the North York Moors National Park are not marked on the latest Ordnance Survey maps; both, for quite different reasons, to help preserve the landscape. No-one can walk on the north-facing escarpment of the high moors of the central Cleveland Hills and fail to notice the ugly scar of the line of the Lyke Wake Walk, a gruelling, 40 mile (64km) bog-trot which crosses the highest and wildest parts of the moors between Osmotherley and Ravenscar. Some 30 years ago the Lyke Wake was conceived by local farmer Bill Cowley. The name comes from one of the oldest dialect verses in the English language, the Lyke Wake Dirge, which perpetuates the idea that, after death, the soul is transported up over the

moors to meet its Maker. This may be a distant echo of the custom among Bronze Age people to bury their dead on the highest points of the moors, evidence of which is indicated by the 3,000 howes, or burial mounds, shown on the map. Bill Cowley's innocent suggestion, first made in *The Dalesman* magazine, was that it should be possible to walk for 40 miles (64km) across the moors in 24 hours 'and never meet a soul'. He later reflected in his official guide: 'I wrote enthusiastically, not knowing what I was letting myself in for.'

The trouble with the Lyke Wake Walk is that it is an ideal length for a really tough challenge walk, and that the moors are crossed by a series of north-south roads which are conveniently placed for support parties to service walkers. The incredible popularity of the Lyke Wake Walk, for which successful 'dirgers' were awarded a 'card of condolence' for completing the route in the allotted time, became a *cause*

The foundations of the Roman road known as Wade's Causeway cross Wheeldale Moor

The stately ruins of Rievaulx Abbey – founded in 1131, it was the earliest Cistercian abbey in the north of England

célèbre in countryside management, as up to 10,000 people a year attempted it. The resultant erosion on the soft, largely peat surface of the moors was appalling, and a great elephant trod of churned-up peat, the width of a road in some places, made a mockery of the fact that some parts were still marked as 'undefined' on older maps. Something had to be done, and the National Park authority, with 1,000 miles (1,600km) of other rights of way to look after in the Park, persuaded the Ordnance Survey and various rambling groups to ignore the route, to stop promoting it and give it a rest – which is why you won't find the Lyke Wake Walk marked on Ordnance Survey maps, or in any National Park publications. It remains the longest I

have ever tackled in a day, but I would not want to submit to its funereal torture again, especially as there is so much more pleasurable walking within the Park.

One of the few exciting moments on the Lyke Wake Walk is the first sight of the famous Fylingdales 'Golf Balls' as you cross the tumulus-topped Simon Howe on Howl Moor. The surreal sight of the three huge, dazzlingly white spheres which house a NATO radar early warning station on the horizon of Fylingdales Moor means that the end of the torture is in sight, and beyond them lies Ravenscar and the sea. But like the Lyke Wake Walk, they are never mentioned on a map, presumably in case the Russians should buy one! The words 'MOD Property' are the only clue to the reason for their painfully obvious presence.

The Golf Balls became so famous that they became a tourist attraction in their own right, and serious attempts were made to have them 'listed' as an ancient monument when it was announced they were to be replaced. Opinions have always been divided as to the merits of the Golf Balls, but no-one seems to favour the gigantic, truncated pyramid which has been erected by the Ministry of Defence in their place. The so-called 'peace dividend' of recent events in Eastern Europe should also surely question the need for structures which were designed to give us the famed 'four minute warning' of the approaching Apocalypse from threatened nuclear missiles across the North Sea.

The Fylingdales Early Warning Station may be the latest addition to the landscape of the North York Moors, but the Moors' story starts between 210 and 145 million years ago, during the Jurassic period. It was then

The pretty village of Hutton-le-Hole, clustered around its green, is one of the showplaces of the Park

North Yorkshire Moors Railway

*T*he delightful North Yorkshire Moors Railway operates on 18 miles (29km) of track between Grosmont and Pickering, and steam trains puff their way up and down the hills and valleys between Easter and the end of October. The line traverses moorland, forest and valley on its way through the North York Moors National Park. Novelist Charles Dickens travelled on this line, and referred to it as 'a quaint old railway'.

The route dates back to 1836, when George Stephenson himself engineered the line for horse-drawn coaches, which in one place had to be hauled up an incline with a rope, counterbalanced by a tank of water. Closed by British Rail in 1965, passenger services were restarted by the preservation society in 1973.

At Grosmont the preserved railway's station adjoins the main British Rail Esk Valley platform, and trains leaving for the south soon plunge into a tunnel. Alongside is the narrow Stephenson-built one, now used for the footpath to the engine sheds. Beyond is a very steep climb at 1 in 49, with fine views to the right before the train enters the steep valley of the Murk Esk. From one of the bridges there is a drop of 100ft (31m)

Popular with steam enthusiasts, the railway is also a pleasant way to see the North Yorkshire countryside

to the cascading water below. At the top of the steepest part of the climb is the pretty village of Goathland. Close at hand is Mallyan Spout waterfall, while there are the remains of a Roman road passing only 2½ miles (4km) away.

Beyond Goathland the valley opens out as the summit is reached, enabling the distinctive giant 'Golf Balls' of the Early Warning Station at Fylingdales to be seen, near where the route of the famous Lyke Wake Walk crosses the railway. The line twists dramatically between towering sandstone cliffs before reaching the forests that can be explored by the tracks that radiate from Newtondale Halt. The next station is Levisham, where iron was once smelted with the aid of local charcoal.

Approaching the terminus at the busy market town of Pickering, ruined lime kilns are a reminder of another local industry. The walls of the castle, set high on the hill above the town, are said to have guarded every medieval king of England.

Trains pass at the pretty station of Goathland

that the sandstones which form the Cleveland and Hambleton Hills were deposited, later to be incised by the deep dales of the tributaries of the River Esk and Derwent flowing north and south. Rivers like the Danby Beck, Great and Little Fryup Becks, Glaisdale Beck and Wheeldale Beck cut short, deeply-incised dales to meet the Esk to the north, while Ryedale, Bilsdale, Bransdale, Farndale and Rosedale are broader, more extensive dales whose rivers flow into the Vale of Pickering to the south. In between are the Upper Jurassic limestone escarpments of the Tabular Hills, between Helmsley and Scarborough, which get their name from their flat-tops and steep, north-facing escarpments standing like sentinels before the moors.

The North Sea continues to wage a constant battle with the Cleveland coastline, making it one of the fastest-eroding in the country. In places the cliffs are being eaten away by the crashing waves at the rate of 3ft (1m) a year, and the average rate of erosion is 3 in (7.6cm) per annum. Only three villages meet the sea, Staithes, Runswick and Robin Hood's Bay, and they all have the feeling of Cornish smuggling villages, with close-packed houses crowding down to the shore. Boulby Cliff, in the northernmost extremity of the Park, is the highest point on the east coast of England at 666ft (202m). Paradoxically, just inland from the towering cliffs, Boulby potash mine with its intrusive chimney boasts

Runswick Bay is one of only three villages on the Park's coastline

the deepest mine shaft in England, 3,750ft (1,143m) deep. Mercifully, due to the more recent geology of the Moors, this is the only form of mineral wealth currently being extracted from the National Park.

In the past, however, sandstone, whinstone and alum were extensively quarried, and at the head of Rosedale the ruined remains of buildings, kilns and the track beds of railways can still be seen high on the empty moor where

the local ironstone beds were mined. In the 1860s there were over 80 ironstone mines in the region, sunk to serve the expanding needs of the Industrial Revolution. The distinctive peak-shape of Roseberry Topping – known as the 'Matterhorn of Cleveland', and perhaps the best-known hill in the Park – is partly due to the collapse of its west face due to the effects of ironstone mining.

Another line of workings along the 900ft (274m) contour of the Cleveland Hills, especially noticeable in Scugdale, shows where the semi-precious Whitby jet – a fossilised conifer wood hugely popular in Victorian days – was extracted.

Settlements in the North York Moors are generally small and nucleated. The main centres are Helmsley, where the National Park authority has its headquarters, and which has a fine square and ruined

Pantile-clad cottages crowd down to the sea at Staithes – a Norse name which means quay or landing place

Steep steps lead up from the harbour at Whitby, a popular centre just outside the Park

12th-century castle, and Pickering, to the east, formerly the centre for the medieval Royal Forest of Pickering and watched over by its own 12th-century castle ruins.

The boundary of these hunting forests, which were never the heavily-wooded areas suggested by the modern interpretation of the name, was often marked by substantial stone crosses high on the moors. These crosses, of which over 30 are named on Ordnance Survey maps, also served as important navigational aids to travellers passing over the bleak and featureless wastes. They have often been given names by local people, such as the 9ft (2.7m) tall Ralph Cross, standing 1,400ft (427m) up on the moors near the head of Rosedale, which was chosen by the National Park authority as its emblem. The cross is more accurately known as

Young Ralph, to distinguish it from Old Ralph, a few hundred yards to the west. Other moorland crosses commemorate Fat Betty, Blue Man i' th' Moss, Percy, Anna, Redman and Job. One of the most interesting and most ancient is Lilla Cross on Lilla Howe, on Fylingdales Moors east of the Golf Balls. It commemorates the loyal henchman of King Edwin of Northumbria who died stopping an assassin's dagger meant for his master. The Romans passed this way also, and Wade's Causeway, crossing Wheeldale Moor near Wheeldale Lodge Youth Hostel, shows the foundations of one of the best-preserved stretches of Roman roads in the north of England.

Pretty villages like Goathland in Eskdale and Hutton-le-Hole at the foot of lovely Farndale cluster around extensive sheep-grazed greens, and the excellent Ryedale Folk Museum at

Hutton-le-Hole has many reconstructed vernacular houses and other interesting exhibits for the visitor to inspect.

A good way of exploring the Moors is to leave your car behind and use the 24 mile (38km) North York Moors Railway which runs steam trains between Grosmont in Eskdale and Pickering, through the spectacular glacial gorge of Newton Dale. Designed by George Stephenson and originally a horse-drawn tramway, the line opened in 1836 but closed under the Beeching axe in 1965. Steam enthusiasts were determined that such a scenic line should re-open, and this was eventually achieved in 1973. The line now carries over 250,000 passengers a year (see page 124–5).

However, perhaps the most impressive man-made features of the North York Moors date back to medieval times, when the area was known as 'Blackamor'. The first people to realise the wealth of the Moors were the monks of the religious orders who subsequently built their beautiful abbeys around the edges. Rievaulx Abbey, founded in 1131 on the wooded banks of the River Rye on land granted by Walter L'Espec of Helmsley Castle is the earliest, and many people believe it to be the most beautiful abbey ruin in Britain. Byland Abbey, just 5 miles (8km) to the south, was transported from Old Byland in 1147 when it was thought that its proximity to Rievaulx was too much of a good thing! It was in the lovely, sacred setting of Rievaulx that Ailred expressed all that is best about the Moors – 'a marvellous freedom from the tumult of the world'.

Looking down onto Robin Hood's Bay from North Cheek, with South Cheek and Beacon Howes in the distance

NORTHUMBERLAND

To the legionary posted to Hadrian's Wall, Northumberland must
have seemed like the end of the world – as indeed it was at the
time. This astonishing manifestation of 2nd-century military
power, which stretched across the neck of England along the crest
of the Great Whin Sill, marked the northernmost extremity of the
Roman Empire and remains a powerful monument to the might
that was Rome. Further north, the great, empty, curlew-haunted
wastes of Northumberland stretch up to the wild and remote
heights of the Cheviots, another perpetual borderland with
Scotland which, although largely peaceful now, shows many signs
of an equally turbulent past.

Previous pages, the Empty Quarter – the view east from Carter Bar, Northumberland

A view of the River Coquet, which rises in the heart of the Cheviots, in Upper Coquetdale

My photographer friend John had plans to seek out and photograph the wild Cheviot Chasm known as the Hen Hole in its winter raiment, and to start with it looked as though we were to be thwarted. Our approach was to be from the remote northern valley of the College Burn (due to the proximity of the Border many physical features in this part of the world have a Scottish ring to them), and to enter the College valley by car – thus avoiding an extra 6 mile (9.6km) hike along the road – the visitor has to obtain a permit from the estate office in the pleasant little market town of Wooler. 'I'm sorry,' said the girl behind the desk, 'there'll be no permits today because of the snow conditions. We don't want to encourage skiers.' Our hearts sank, but

after we had explained we weren't going skiing, and that John had travelled all the way from Wiltshire to take these photographs in the snow, she relented and we were issued with our pass.

The approach to the College valley from Hethpool was dramatic as snow-clad hills with Scottish-sounding names like Hare Law and Coldburn Hill crowded in. We passed the odd little oak wood of Hethpoolbell Wood, known locally as the Collingwood Oaks because they were planted by a hero of Trafalgar, Admiral Lord Collingwood, to provide more timber for the 'wooden walls of England'. On the opposite bank, on the slopes of White Hill, we noted a fine set of lynchets – medieval cultivation terraces – outlined in the snow, and

The remains of an Iron Age hut circle high on Humbleton Hill, in the north of the Park, looking towards Yeavering Bell

the map showed in Gothic lettering the remains of many other field systems, enclosures, homesteads and settlements on the now deserted hills above.

Hethpool, like many of these Border villages, boasts a ruined pele tower, a fortified house built for defence against the frequent destructive raids of the infamous border reivers. For something like 300 years, from the late 13th to the mid-l6th century, this area of the Border was in a state of constant internecine warfare, which took no account of nationality or social class. Reiving, which gave two significant words to our language, bereave and blackmail, was not so much a nuisance, more a way of life. At the time it was said that no man could walk abroad unarmed in safety, no one could sleep secure, and neither beast nor cattle could be left unguarded.

When a laird's lady brought a plate holding a pair of spurs to the table, he knew the larder was empty and it was time once again to 'shake loose the border'.

In other Border villages, such as the classic example of Elsdon in Redesdale, the stone-built houses are clustered around a broad village green, much in the manner of wagons round a camp fire in a Western film. This was so that the cattle and livestock of the villagers could be brought into the green and defended at times of attack. Elsdon has perhaps the finest pele tower in the area, as well as one of the best examples of a Norman motte-and-bailey castle at the Mote Hills, north of the village centre.

As we parked by the shepherd's cottage at Mounthooly, at the end of the twisting, single-track road, the

The charming little market town of Wooler is the key to the College Valley, and the heart of the Cheviots

brooding, almost oppressive silence of these ancient hills first struck us and it was hard to believe that they once echoed with the sound of steel-bonneted horsemen heralding murder and mayhem, rape and pillage.

We set off through the snow, leaving the dark, ugly, regimented plantations of conifer belts behind, and slowly climbed into the heart of the hills. We passed several circular sheep pens, a Northumbrian speciality known here by the Old Norse word *stell*, as we headed for the Border Ridge on the horizon. The nick in the skyline ahead, Red Cribs, was mentioned in 1597 as 'Gribbheade, a passage and hyeway for the theefe', and was undoubtedly used by reivers bringing home their ill-gotten gains. As the track leading up to Red Cribs steepened, the awesome cleft of the Hen Hole opened up to our left and we looked straight into the icy heart of the Cheviot, whose snowy 2,678ft (816m) summit towered above. The Hen Hole is thought to have been cut through the volcanic granite of the

Cheviot by the immensely powerful meltwaters of an Ice Age glacier. The College Burn still cascades down its gloomy depths in a fine series of waterfalls which, during our visit, were cloaked in curtains of blue ice and watched over by impressive cornices of snow; perfect for John's photographs.

The Cheviot Hills, smooth-sloped and capped by notorious peat bogs which are the bane of Pennine wayfarers on the last lap of their 250-mile (400km) journey to Kirk Yetholm, just across the Border, form the highest ground in the 405-square-mile (1,049 sq km) Northumberland National Park. The Park, designated in 1956, was a bit of a hybrid as the planners sought to link the obvious attractions of Hadrian's Wall with the Cheviots 50 miles (80km) to the north, beyond the vast Redesdale Army Ranges.

About a fifth of the National Park is an active training area administered by the Ministry of Defence, and walkers in the central area around Redesdale and the Coquet valley must be beware of live-firing activities (advertised in information centres and by the flying of a red flag) before they set out on the hills. Out of place as this may seem, in a strange way the Army is only perpetuating an age-old, almost traditional, land use in these remote hills.

Yeavering Bell, just north of the Cheviot on a twin-topped 1,180ft (359m) outlier of the main range, is the most extensive of several hillforts dating from the Iron Age which stud these hills. When the Romans arrived, however, they imposed their military might on the area in such a way that there is still tangible evidence of their

The Vicar of Elsdon's pele tower, first mentioned in 1415, is one of the finest in the Borders

Hadrian's Wall

*Making the most of natural
landscape features, the wall
crosses Cuddy's Crag*

The barrier across Britain between Solway and Tyne was built because the Emperor Hadrian wanted to separate the Romans from the barbarians. Roman soldiers, who were also skilled engineers and craftsmen, began work on the wall in AD122. It took just over seven years to complete and, huge though the wall was, it formed only a part of Hadrian's complete defence system. On the north side a steep ditch ran parallel to the wall, and to the south a flat-bottomed ditch with earth ramparts built up on either side, known as the vallum. As part of the same system, there were also small, regularly spaced forts and watchtowers down the Cumbrian coast, and a Roman port on the Tyne at South Shields.

On the wall itself at intervals of 1,620yds (1,481m) – or one Roman mile – there were milecastles, which held up to 64 men and had gateways to the north and south. Turrets, used as watchtowers, were built between the milecastles and, in addition to this, there were 17 forts placed strategically on or near the wall, manned by troops or cavalry. All together the wall garrison consisted of about 15,000 men.

Although the wall has been virtually derelict since the end of the 4th century, the surviving remains are nevertheless extensive and very impressive, not least because of their beautiful setting. Working across from the east, the first visible remains are at South Shields, where parts of a fort are preserved.

The wall was plundered in 1781 for the building of military roads, so little survives on the stretch to Brunton, where there is a fine section of wall and a well-preserved turret. Beyond the remains of the fort at Chesters, the wall rises to 1,230ft (375m), following the geological ridge of the Whin Sill. The central sector of the wall begins here and it runs through magnificent wild countryside. Lonely moors stretch away to the north with the hills of south Scotland and north Northumberland in the distance, while to the south lies the fertile valley of the Tyne.

Heading west again, only grass-covered ramparts remain of Carrawburgh fort, but a temple of Mithras has been preserved near by.

The military road leaves the wall at Shield-on-the-Wall, and next comes Housesteads, the best preserved and most exciting of the Roman forts. Its ramparts and gateways have been very well preserved, and the granaries, headquarters, commandant's house, hospital, latrines, some barracks and civilian settlements have been uncovered. The bodies of a man and woman were found beneath the floor of one of these, the point of a sword embedded in the man's ribs.

Further along the wall is the fort at Chesterholm, and the wall continues along the Whin Sill to Cawfields and the fort at Greatchesters, with its ramparts, two gateways, barracks and underground strong-room. After this the wall is not so well preserved, but at Walltown a lone turret still survives. After Birdoswald the land becomes gentler, though no less beautiful, and red sandstone takes over from the limestone. Since the wall has provided building materials in the past, few remains of it are visible beyond Walton village, except the ditch and earthworks.

The Hadrian's Wall Walk covers 74 miles (118km) from Wallsend to Bowness-on-Solway. At the moment the general line of the wall can be walked following footpaths and long stretches of road, and the Countryside Commission is preparing a complete Hadrian's Wall National Trail.

The remains of the fort at Housesteads give visitors a good idea of Roman life on the wall

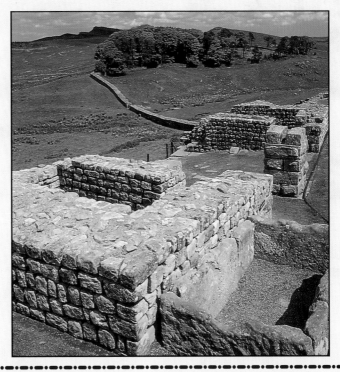

Northumberland Wall country – looking towards Crag Lough and Winshields Crag, the highest point of Hadrian's Wall

presence nearly 2,000 years later. It was in AD120, according to his biographer, that the Emperor Hadrian gave instructions for the building of a wall across the narrowest point of his colony of Britannia 'to separate the Romans from the barbarians'. Incredibly, the 73 mile (117km) wall between the Solway and the Tyne took the workforce of 10,000 men only eight years to build, and it remains the most impressive example of Roman military architecture in north-western Europe. Fifteen miles (24km) of the best-preserved stretch of the Wall form the southern boundary

of the National Park as it follows the line of the natural defence formed by the escarpment of the Great Whin Sill, an igneous intrusion forming upstanding crags of basalt. The best-known section of the Wall is around the fort at Housesteads, where there is an excellent visitor information centre.

With milecastles placed at every Roman mile, a dozen forts of the distinctive playing-card shape found at Housesteads, and an associated 20ft (6m) wide *vallum* – a sort of military no-go zone – the wall was manned by a force of 10,000 men,

villages; many of the most interesting recent finds of Wall material have been found in the farms and barns of neighbouring farms.

The constant robbery of this great monument deeply offended one of the Wall's earliest and most delightful supporters. In 1801, 78-year-old William Hutton, a Birmingham antiquary and businessman, walked the 600 miles (960km) from his home city to the Wall, then walked along the length of it and back again. In the hugely entertaining account of his adventure that Hutton wrote afterwards, he harangued a group of workmen demolishing a section of the Wall at Planetrees, saying that their master was: '...putting an end to the most noble monument of Antiquity in the whole Island'. Hutton claimed to be the first man to travel the length of the Wall and back, but he is likely to be followed by many others when the Hadrian's Wall National Trail is created.

Beyond the Wall to the north-west lies the huge expanse of the Border

A classic view of Hadrian's Wall, looking towards Housesteads Crag

most of whom would have been auxiliary soldiers from all over the Empire. When standing on the remains of this still impressive frontier at a spot like Cuddy's Crag, or Steel Rigg on the central part of the Wall, it is easy to feel something of the isolation and fear that must have been in the minds of those soldiers as they nervously patrolled the ramparts.

Hadrian's Wall was over-run by invading forces on several occasions before being finally abandoned at the end of the 4th century, after which it became a convenient quarry for building-stone for local farms and

and Kielder Forest, the most extensive man-made landscape in Europe. The River North Tyne was impounded to create Kielder Water, which is as big as Ullswater in the Lake District and the largest man-made lake in Europe. It lies just outside the National Park boundary.

The names of the hills in this central section of the National Park give a clue to their violent history: Bloodybush Edge, Oh Me Edge, Deadwater Fell and Gallow Law. Close to the headquarters of the Army training ground west of Elsdon, on the A696 at Otterburn, a simple stone obelisk, half hidden in a small plantation of firs, commemorates one of the most famous and bloody clashes between English and Scottish Forces. Percy's Cross is named after the leader of the English forces, Sir Henry Percy, who

A winter's day at Catcleugh Reservoir, at the head of Redesdale

was defeated by an inferior force of Scots led by James, Earl of Douglas, at the Battle of Otterburn in 1388. But Douglas's victory was won at enormous cost when his fateful pre-battle premonition, recorded by Sir Walter Scott in *The Battle of Otterburn*, was fulfilled:

> But I hae dream'd a dreary dream,
> Beyond the Isle of Skye;
> I saw a dead man win a fight,
> And I think that man was I.

The upland area to the east of Otterburn and the valley of the Rede is locally known as the 'Black Country' because of the dark, heather-clad sandstone hills broken by steep crags. The Simonside and Harbottle Hills near Rothbury form a separate and distinct group, much

more typically Pennine in their character.

Many enigmatic carvings, known as 'cup-and-ring' marks, have been identified on the sandstone boulders which litter the slopes of the Simonside Hills. These intricate designs are thought to date from the Bronze Age, but no-one has yet come up with a satisfactory answer as to why they were carved.

The view northwards from the high escarpment of Simonside extends across the broad, patchwork-quilt landscape of the Coquet valley towards the distant, often snow-covered heights of the Cheviots. These higher granite summits are known as the 'White Country' by local people, which again accurately reflects the predominate colour of the vegetation. The lower slopes of the smoothly

contoured hills are mostly clothed in pale tawny moor grass and grazed by huge flocks of Roman-nosed Cheviot sheep. It is here, on these rolling, grass-clad summits where the views can extend northwards far into Scotland, and east and west from the North to the Irish Sea, that the true freedom of Northumberland can be experienced. It was well expressed by the great Northumberland-born historian, G M Trevelyan:

Although outside the Park, Kielder Water – the largest man-made lake in Europe – is a popular attraction

In Northumberland alone, both heaven and earth are seen; we walk all day on long ridges, high enough to give far views of moor and valley, and the sense of solitude far below...It is the land of far horizons...

THE BROADS

The Broads is the newest member of the National Park family, and it has the youngest landscape. But if anyone had suggested just 40 years ago, when the first National Park was being designated, that this enchanted area of mysterious, misty fens and slow, winding waterways was anything other than natural, no-one would have believed them. However, we now know that this entire network of dykes and broads on the borders of Suffolk and Norfolk is entirely man-made – and it is none the less beautiful for that. The area was given long overdue protection when it was created a National Park in all but name in 1989.

The white-sailed Boardman's Windmill on the River Ant, near How Hill

Previous pages, a typical Broadland scene – the windpump, on the Berney Arms Reach which crosses Reedham Marshes

The cormorants sat motionless on the windmill, silhouetted like two metal, cut-out weathervanes, one on the topmost edge of the sail and the other perched precariously on the tail vane. There was no danger that their belvedere would be disturbed, for the weather on that winter's day at How Hill, in the heart of the Broads, was misty, damp and eerily calm. The sinister black shapes of the cormorants seemed to remain in their commanding position for most of the seminar which I was attending at the How Hill environmental centre for the Broads, adding to the impression of their permanence.

The view from the Sun Room at How Hill was both a constant distraction and an inspiration during the long meetings, for, from its lofty heights – lofty, that is, for the low-lying Broads – the vista extended over the winding River Ant, the waving, tawny reedmarshes of Reedham, Clayrack and Bisley, and down to the red-brick towermill at Turf Fen. It was this glorious panorama which

Hill is still the highest point of the Broads National Park.

First recorded as 'Haugr', or 'Haugh Hill', meaning high point, it owes its name to the Viking invaders from Denmark who first nosed the inquisitive prows of their proud longships into the shallow staithe below the hill on the River Ant during the 9th century. The word *staithe* is found regularly along the east coast of England between Northumberland and Norfolk, and is pure Danish, meaning a quay, or landing point for ships. The view from How Hill was beautifully described by Walter White in a guidebook to Eastern England published in 1865:

> ... a big knoll, thickly covered with oat-grass, from the top of which we had a pleasant view, and enjoyed the scent of elder blossom with which we had become familiar; broad reedy flats, pastures of various colour, coarse swamps, bright patches of poppies, irregular patches of water, windmills and dykes, and the narrow stream repeating its lazy curves across the vast level.

The busy quayside at Wroxham, on the River Bure, is a major centre for boat hire on the Broads

attracted Edward Boardman, the Norwich architect, and inspired him to build the charming Edwardian, reed-thatched and gabled house of How Hill as the family home.

How Hill itself is a prominent knoll of sand and gravel laid down in the outwash from a melting ice sheet during the Ice Ages. Once part of a much larger plateau, it was reduced to its present size by the abrasive action of the same glacial meltwaters which signalled the end of the Ice Age. At a mere 40ft (12m) above the sea, How

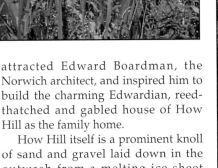

Hickling, on Hickling Broad, is one of the quieter backwaters

of the *Papilionidae* family, more usually found in the tropics, and makes a magnificent sight as it feeds on the flowers of campion and milk parsley.

During a break in the seminar we wandered down to How Hill staithe, inspecting the charming little former eel-catchers' cottage of Toad Hole on the way. This reed-thatched, red-brick two-up, two-down cottage, hidden away in the willows, has been faithfully reconstructed and furnished in traditional style by the National Park authority, and one half expects

He was describing a typical Broads landscape as it was before the invasion of tourism that began with the arrival of the railway in the 1870s.

But those marshy levels which ring How Hill remain some of the finest reedmarshes in Britain, and the home of rare, water-loving wildlife. Inhabitants include the mercurial hen harrier, which can often be seen quartering the reedbeds on floating, buoyant wings; the elusive bittern, whose booming notes echo across the marshes in the spring; the handsome bearded tit or reedling, and the more dowdy reed warbler, which builds its neat, circular nest using living reedstems as supports.

The huge wintering flocks of teal, wigeon, coot and redshank were the Norfolk wildfowlers' stock-in-trade in days gone by, and the spectacular swallowtail butterfly, Britain's biggest, still beats its showy way across the fen in high summer, attracting lepidopterists from all over the country. It is the only British member

to see Ratty and Mole appearing round the corner.

Moored up at the staithe was *Hathor*, a traditional Norfolk wherry sail boat. These broad-beamed, black-sailed wherries were the main form of cargo transport on the Broads for 200 years, but now the 23-ton *Hathor*, built at nearby Reedham in 1905, plies a charter trade for tourists along with a handful of other such craft. On board was skipper Peter Bower, passing the time of day with Eric Edwards, one of the last reed-cutters still employed on the Broads. The top-quality Norfolk reed is still in high demand for thatching all over the country, and Eric was looking forward to a busy harvest.

It took the combined research skills of a geographer, a botanist and a geomorphologist to finally crack the code which explained the creation of the Broads. Until then, less than 40 years ago, the enchanted, wet wilderness of the Broads had been regarded as an entirely natural landscape.

In fact, the 117 square miles (303 sq km) of the Norfolk Broads National Park, centred around three major

Hickling Broad, with its wide expanse of reedbeds, is a National Nature Reserve and a haven for wildlife

rivers, the Bure, the Yare and the Waveney, and their tributaries, the Ant, the Thurne and the Chet, which all meander down to the sea at Great Yarmouth, have been said to represent the greatest human modifications ever made to the natural landscape of this country. Geomorphologists had noted from borings that the original sides of the water-filled basins of the Broads were almost vertical and cut directly through the natural peat of the valley floors. Also, some Broads contained narrow, parallel peninsulas of peat, and islands whose sides were also steeply sloping or vertical. All this pointed to the fact that they were man-made; but where was the historical evidence? The answer to that question came from historians carefully sifting through the records of St Benet's Abbey, on the banks of the River Bure at Holme. The lonely, romantic ruins of this Benedictine monastery (a favourite subject for Victorian artists) are dominated by the 18th-century, round, red-brick towermill built inside the gatehouse. St Benet's, one of the most important historic sites in the Broads, probably dates from the 9th century, but was rebuilt and

The 'Helter Skelter House' at Potter Heigham is the truncated remains of a Yarmouth fairground ride

endowed with three manors by King Canute in AD1020.

The records showed that from the 12th century onwards certain areas in Hoveton parish were set aside for peat-digging, and in one year alone no fewer than a million turves were cut. This large-scale extraction, mainly for fuel, went on continuously for over two centuries, and by the early 14th century the cathedral priory at nearby Norwich alone was using nearly 400,000 turves annually from the area we now know as the Broads.

The total area excavated by those medieval peat-diggers has been estimated at about 2,600 acres (1,052ha), and the transformation of the 12ft (4m) deep peat-diggings to Broads resulted from gradual flooding from the 13th century onwards. At about this time there was a very slight change in the relative levels of the land and sea, and coastal and low-lying areas became increasingly at risk from flooding. Although there were some attempts to dredge peat under-water, using a special rake known as a dydle, by the 15th century working had become so difficult that peat-cutting was no longer profitable and had been abandoned.

Since then, the shallow lakes have gradually been infilled with dead vegetation and sediment. Tithe maps of the 1840s show an area of nearly 3,000 acres (1,214ha) of open water, whereas today's figure is more like half that total.

Until recently, the waters of the Broads supported a wide variety of water plants which form the basis of

Another individualist's home on the River Thurne at Potter Heigham

the aquatic food chain and in turn support a great variety of insects, small animals and fish. But by the 1950s a significant change had begun to occur, and the waterways became increasingly choked by a luxuriant growth of underwater plants and algae.

The reason for this change was that there had been an enormous increase in the nutrient levels of the water, due to effluent from sewage treatment works and the run-off from the increased application of fertiliser on adjacent farmland. The result was that the formerly crystal-clear waters of the

Broads were turned into a murky pea-soup by the floating algae – a process known to scientists as eutrophication.

The Broads authority has taken steps to halt this process by pumping out the enriched mud from the bottom of some Broads by suction dredging. The results, in places like Cockshoot Dyke and Cockshoot Broad, have been very encouraging, with a dramatic improvement in water quality and the re-establishment of submerged water plants such as waterlily, hornwort and bladderwort.

The 125 miles (200km) of lock-free navigable rivers and Broads in the

A boathouse at Hickling, thatched with locally-grown Norfolk reed

National Park make it one of the most intensively used inland waterways in Europe, and it has been estimated that there were more than 2,000 hire cruisers on the Broads in the mid-1970s. Some 200,000 holidaymakers now use weekly-let motor cruisers annually, and this is also a cause for concern to the Broads authority as the wash from motorised pleasure craft can break up the reed mats on the banks of the Broads, and eventually the banks themselves can be washed away. Artificial bank protection, the imposition of speed limits on boating, the isolation of certain stretches of

bank, and research into hull design are among the solutions currently being investigated.

In total, the Broads National Park receives over three million annual visitors, most of whom come to enjoy the unspoiled beauty of Broads, dykes and fens, the wet, tangled alder carr woodlands, and the wide expanses of grazing marshes under those vast East Anglian skies. Halvergate Marshes, just to the west of Great Yarmouth and bordering Breydon Water, could be said to be the birthplace of the Broads National Park, for in 1985 it became the site of the experiment which was to result in the first Environmentally Sensitive Area (ESA) in England. Here, farmers are paid to manage the extensive, windmill-dotted marshes by traditional grazing methods, and this should conserve their unique features for posterity.

When the idea of National Parks in Britain was being discussed in the 1940s, the eminent biologist Julian Huxley wrote from Paris saying that he could not imagine a group of British National Parks being set up which did not include the Broads. It took 40 years to happen, but now the Broads – that 'last enchanted land' – is an integral, important and very special member of Britain's National Park family.

The ruins of St Benet's Abbey, on the River Bure near Ludham, where the secret of the Broads' creation was revealed

NEW NATIONAL PARKS

THE NEXT NATIONAL PARKS ?

A New Forest pony and foal graze peacefully, in a scene typical of Britain's latest proposed National Park

If there's one thing that the New Forest – the latest area to be granted the status of a National Park – is not, it's 'new'. Most National Park designations date from the 1950s, but the one notable exception is the New Forest which was 'designated' in AD1079, when William the Conqueror first set aside, with a strict set of laws for the protection of game, what he called his 'Nova Foresta'.

The 145 square miles (376 sq km) between Southampton Water and Salisbury Plain merited two full pages in William's famous Domesday survey and the miracle is that, nine centuries later, the description of infertile woodland and furzy waste where William of Normandy hunted his beloved deer still holds true today.

The New Forest has been described as the largest area of uncultivated lowland landscape in North-West Europe, and is still mostly Crown property, administered by the Forestry Commission. The Commission's enlightened policies, especially with regard to the 'Ancient and Ornamental' woodlands, has done much to safeguard this amazing remnant of medieval greenwood: the commons are administered by the ancient New Forest Verderers.

This commendable record of forest management must have influenced the Government in its recent announcement which gave the New Forest the equivalent status of a National Park. Administered by a re-formed Heritage Area Committee, and jointly funded by local and central Government, the new body will have the same responsibilities as a National Park authority, but without its control over development, and planning powers. For many conservationists this is unsatisfactory, and the Council for National Parks has repeated the call for real National Park status to be conferred on the New Forest. However, John Dower would not have excluded the New Forest in his priority list for National Parks in 1945 had he not been reasonably satisfied that it was already in safe hands with the Forestry Commission. He attached the same kind of proviso to the South Downs, where he thought the local authorities would make adequate provision for conservation and recreation. Nevertheless, although the South Downs of East and West Sussex are already an Area of Outstanding Natural Beauty, local authorities in the area have mounted a vigorous campaign for National Park status. It could be argued that areas like the Downs are under the greatest pressure, not only from development and recreation, but from widespread agricultural 'improvement', although the withdrawal of cereal subsidies from Europe has eased the threat to the precious downland that remains.

Apart from the Broads, our present National Parks are mostly of an upland character, largely because the original definition of a National Park referred to 'relatively wild' country and because, generally speaking, less harmful change has taken place in the uplands.

To redress the balance, however, further lowland National Parks have been suggested over the years. These include the Somerset Levels, still threatened by agricultural drainage schemes; the sylvan Wye valley; the beech-hung Chiltern Hills; the Shropshire Hills; and the rolling, honey-stoned Cotswold Hills, one of the largest existing AONBs.

Where the South Downs meet the sea – the Seven Sisters, near Seaford

In 1974 the Countryside Commission recommended the designation of a Cambrian Mountains National Park in central Wales, but local opposition among farmers and landowners was so strong that it was eventually rejected by the Welsh Office. However, surely the lonely hills of Radnor and Pumlumon Fawr, source of the Severn and Wye, and the mellow, reservoired hills of the Elan valley deserve better protection than their present Environmentally Sensitive Area (ESA) status?

Another recently designated AONB which merits the greater protection and resources that National Park status would give is the North Pennines, between the Yorkshire Dales and Hadrian's Wall and Northumberland. The North Pennines AONB was confirmed in 1988 only after a long and hard-fought public inquiry, but many people believe the lovely hills and dales of Teesdale, Weardale, Allendale and the Vale of Eden, known to the tourist boards as 'England's Last Wilderness' and including such scenic highlights as High Force and Cauldron Snout, Cross Fell (the highest point of the Pennines), and the wilds of Stainmore, deserve the greater recognition and support which comes from National Park designation. With the possible inclusion also of the South Pennines, between the Peak and the Yorkshire Dales and known to

Craig Goch Reservoir, in the Elan valley, within the proposed Cambrian Mountains National Park

Dower as 'the industrial Pennines', such a designation would create an almost continuous National Park along the 250 mile (400km) length of the Pennines. As well as affording protection to the landscape, the area would provide much-needed recreational opportunities for the inhabitants of the industrial northern cities.

Apart from the need for more National Parks (Scotland is dealt with separately in the next chapter), there are several anomalies in the present National Park boundaries which many people believe should be rectified. The northern Howgill Fells were, by some inexplicable bureaucratic oversight, excluded

from the Yorkshire Dales National Park and should surely receive the same recognition as the rest of that noble range of hills. A similar anomaly puts half of the smooth-sloped Cheviot Hills within the Northumberland National Park and the other half lying unprotected across the Border in Scotland. It would also seem common sense to include the lovely, wooded, limestone hills of the Quantocks in Somerset within the Exmoor National Park, as the Hobhouse Report recommended way back in 1947.

Cauldron Snout, on the Pennine Way in Upper Teesdale, in the North Pennines

An interesting development in recent years has been the way that, as larger countries have run out of real wilderness areas, they have turned to British National Parks as models of how conservation can take place in lived-in, working landscapes. The National Park movement started in Britain, and it looks like it could still provide the 'greenprint' for the future.

SCOTLAND

ALL OR NOTHING ?

*F*ew people would dispute the fact that the finest wilderness areas in Britain are north of the Border, in Scotland. Yet on the surface it seems a strange paradox that, some 40 years after National Parks were first designated in England and Wales, there are still none in Scotland. To look for the reasons for this apparent anomaly we need to go back into the complicated history of countryside conservation and access in Britain, which developed quite differently on both sides of the Border.

By strange irony, John Muir – one of the greatest pioneers of the original American National Park movement – was a Scot, born in Dunbar, and the first Parliamentary attempt to gain walkers legally-protected access to mountain and moorland in Britain a century ago was prompted by the deteriorating access situation in Scotland. This followed the barbarous Highland Clearances, the introduction of vast sheep farms, and the increasing financial importance to landowners of deer stalking. When the Scottish Liberal MP James Bryce, later Lord Bryce, President of the Alpine Club and Ambassador to the United States, and an experienced mountaineer, introduced his Access to Mountains (Scotland) Bill in 1884, it received cross-party support, prompting a thundering leader in *The Times*, and elicited supportive petitions from many Scottish cities and burghs.

But both this Bill and a successor four years later fell by the wayside, as did several other attempts at similar legislation, and today Scottish hill-goers enjoy a jealously guarded *de facto* right of access to most of the Highlands.

Ironically again, the first recorded mention of National Parks in Parliament, in 1929, also had a specifically Scottish reference. In a question to the Commissioner of Works, a Mr Macpherson called attention to the project 'of securing for the nation in perpetuity some area in the Cairngorm range or elsewhere in

Mists wreath The Three Sisters in Glen Coe, with Aonach Dubh prominent on the left

Looking across the ancient pines of Loch Maree towards the peak of Slioch, in the wilds of Wester Ross

Scotland for the free and unfettered use of the public and as a sanctuary for birds and animals'. The result was the setting up of a committee under Christopher (later Lord) Addison which, for the first time, considered the idea of National Parks in Great Britain. The Committee concluded that, while National Parks based on the American model were impossible in overcrowded Britain, there was, never the less, an 'enviable' opportunity to conserve the best of our countryside.

But when John Dower produced the blueprint for our current National Parks system in England and Wales in his 1945 Report, his terms of reference specifically excluded Scotland. He did say, however, that it was 'exceedingly desirable' that there should be National Parks in Scotland, at a rate of not less than one to three of those in England and Wales:

The mountain masses of the Highlands, with their glens and lochs, are far larger and more continuously wild than any corresponding areas south of the Border; and (in my opinion) at least two selected Highland areas of ample size should become Scottish National Parks simultaneously with the establishment of the first six English and Welsh National Parks.

On the roof of Arctic Britain – looking towards Ben Macdui from Cairn Gorm

A Scottish National Parks Survey Committee under Sir Douglas Ramsay was set up in the same year and identified five possible areas which, when it was decided in 1951 not to apply the 1949 National Parks and Access to the Countryside Act to Scotland, became 'National Park Direction Areas'. These areas gave rather woolly planning safeguards to Loch Lomond and the Trossachs; Ben Nevis, Glen Coe and the Black Mount; Glen Affric, Glen Cannich and Strath Farrar; the Cairngorms; and Torridon, Loch Maree and Loch Broom. They were later embraced within 40 'National Scenic Areas' proposed by the Countryside Commission for Scotland (CCS) in 1978 as 'areas of national scenic significance' that were considered to be 'of unsurpassed attractiveness which must be conserved as part of our national heritage'.

In one of its last acts before it was absorbed with the Nature Conservancy Council, Scotland into the new Government advisory agency, Scottish Natural Heritage, the CCS produced a controversial last stab at the National Parks question with its Report, The Mountain Areas of Scotland, published in 1990. Four National Park areas were proposed (corresponding quite closely to the original National Park Direction Areas), in Loch Lomond and the Trossachs; Ben Nevis, Glen Coe and the Black Mount; the Cairngorms; and Wester Ross, including Torridon and Loch Maree. The Parks were to be zoned according to the Continental model, with mountain wilderness cores where there would be a presumption against any development. Administration would be by independent planning boards or joint local authority committees, along the lines of the existing English and Welsh Parks.

But the proposals were widely perceived as being hasty and ill-conceived by many conservationists, mountain users and landowners, and the Government's response was to shelve the report and, in the short term, to rely instead on voluntary agreements with landowners and local authorities in new National Heritage Areas regarding conservation and access matters. While most objectors were not against the principle of National Parks in Scotland, they felt the CCS plan was seriously flawed. The objections included the imposition of yet another level of bureaucracy in the Scottish countryside, and wildland enthusiasts feared the very use of the term 'National Park' would be misunderstood and encourage more tourists to venture into sensitive areas. The problems of access, land ownership and the socio-economic aspects of designation were largely ignored. Many Scottish hill-goers believed that it was invidious to pick out certain areas of the Highlands for special protection, and that effective national planning control strategies, not 'pocket protection', were the answer.

While the arguments rage on, however, Scotland's landscape heritage remains imperfectly protected, and there is no doubt that some areas have suffered. These include Aviemore in the Cairngorms (large-scale tourism development); in the Flow Country of Sutherland and the Southern Uplands (inappropriate afforestation); and in many previously unspoiled lochs on the west coast, where the uncontrolled and often unsightly cages of fish farms now sometimes pollute both the scenery and the water. Other threats looming just around the corner include plans for massive 'super-quarries', taking aggregates from coastal sites.

But Scottish Natural Heritage must be given time to prove itself as an appropriate and effective guardian of this precious resource, and the experience gained over the last 40 years cannot be ignored. National Parks may still come into being in Scotland, but if they do they will have to be designed to meet the special needs and conditions which exist north of the Border.

On the bonny, bonny banks of Loch Lomond, Britain's largest lake

INDEX